Save That Dog!

Save That Dog!

Everything you need to
know about adopting a
purebred rescue dog

Liz Palika

**HOWELL
BOOK
HOUSE
NEW YORK**

Howell Book House
A Simon & Schuster Macmillan Company
1633 Broadway
New York, NY 10019

Library of Congress Cataloging-in-Publication Data
Palika, Liz, 1954-
    Save that dog! : everything you need to know about adopting a purebred rescue
dog / Liz Palika.
        p.   cm.
    Includes bibliographical references.
    ISBN 0-87605-737-7
    1. Dogs   2. Dog adoption.   3. Dog rescue.   I. Title.
SF427.P18   1997
636.7'0832—dc21   96-30038
                                               CIP

Manufactured in the United States of America

99 98 97   9 8 7 6 5 4 3 2

Book Design: George McKeon
Cover Design: Andrea Weinreb
Photography: All photos by Liz Palika, except where noted.

Acknowledgments

Many people helped make this a successful project. Lori Levin, president of Project BREED, was very helpful and provided me with the updated version of the directories. Terry Albert and Lyn Bingham of Seattle Purebred Dog Rescue answered all of my many (and I'm sure sometimes annoying) questions.

Many rescue groups shared sample copies of their forms, contracts and procedures, shared their newsletters, and told me of successful (and sometimes, unsuccessful) adoptions. Thanks go to Yankee Golden Retriever Rescue, Yankee Siberian Husky, GRCS-DC Golden Retriever Rescue Service, Golden Retriever Club of San Diego County Inc., German Shepherd Rescue, Collie Humane Care, Australian Shepherd Club of America, Aussie Rescue & Placement Helpline and Greyhound Pets of America. And there were more! I want to thank, too, all of the people who sent me stories and photos of their adopted dogs; I wish I could have used all of your stories!

I also want to thank Dominique DeVito, who was instrumental in the initial stages of this book. She saw what I wanted to do and helped me shape it. Thanks, Dominique. Thanks, too, to my new editor, Beth Adelman. Here's to a long and prosperous partnership!

Table of Contents

Introduction

Watachie was my third rescue dog. He had been abandoned as a very young puppy in a rural area and had, by our best guess, survived by eating road kill. Infested with internal and external parasites, skinny, wary and sick, I adopted him from the rescue group only after they warned me about the special care he would need. Little did I know that the time and money I spent nursing him back to health would be one of the best investments of my life.

Obviously a purebred German Shepherd, Watachie was an intelligent, quick-thinking and fun-loving puppy and quickly became my best friend. Even though I had owned dogs before, I had never had a relationship with a dog the way I did with this one. We had a lot of fun together, traveling and camping and investigating the various dog activities and dog sports. Watachie learned to pull a wagon. He enjoyed Frisbees and went on to compete in our state final competitions two years in a row, a rare achievement for a big German Shepherd. He was a certified air scenting search and rescue dog with several finds to his credit. He competed in Obedience, earning his titles with several High in Trial awards, and went on to earn Obedience Trial Championship points with several High Combined awards, stopping short of earning his OTCh because of health problems.

Watachie died when he was eight years old, much too young, leaving me with a gaping hole in my heart. But I believe he accomplished what he set out to do. Because of Watachie, I learned to enjoy dog obedience training, I started teaching dog obedience classes, and I learned how much fun some of the various dog sports could be. Because of the fun we had together, dogs became my life's work; my joy and my profession.

Thanks, Watachie, I miss you still.

Love, Liz

··

PART I

Purebred Dog Rescue

CHAPTER 1

• •

Too Many Dogs Without Homes

It has been estimated that less than 30 percent of all puppies born today will spend their entire life with their original owner or original purchaser (not the breeder). Using the current ownership estimates of over 50 million dogs in the United States, that means more than 35 million dogs will be looking for new homes, will be abandoned or will be euthanized in shelters.

And dog ownership is on the rise. In a recent issue of the *Journal of the American Veterinary Medical Association,* R. Nassar stated that by the year 2000 there are projected to be more than 60 million dogs in the United States.

Every dog owner should be aware of the millions of dogs killed each year in animal shelters. In one medium sized (60,000 people) Southwestern city, more than 250 dogs are euthanized each month. Spread those figures over the entire country and it becomes a national shame. "More dogs die because they are unwanted than from accidents or any single disease," according to Drs. Gary Patronek and Larry Glickman in a January 1995 article in *Dog Fancy.*

The numbers of dogs euthanized each year is based, in part, on the fact that there are more dogs than there are responsible, permanent homes for them. Dog owners who refuse to take responsibility for their dogs have created problems other than just high euthanasia statistics, as well. People don't like to hear about thousands of dogs being killed annually; it reflects badly on all dog owners and has affected how all people, including our elected officials, regard dogs and their owners.

Never has owning a dog been such a negative thing. Today, signs forbidding dogs access to public areas, including beaches and parks, are seen all over the country. Anti-dog legislation is more prevalent now than it has ever been. Legal issues, overpopulation and irresponsible dog ownership are discussed frequently in dog magazines, and the American Kennel Club has a whole department dedicated to canine legislation. This could be the dawn of a new age of dog ownership and it's not a positive one, especially not for purebred dogs.

Mainstream publications have focused on the problem, too. The December 1994 issue of *Time* magazine had as its cover feature an article titled "That's No Way to Treat a Dog." In it the author, Michael Lemonick, discussed not only the numbers of purebred dogs that are euthanized every year, but also some of the genetic defects resulting from consumer fads and poor breeding practices.

Many people concerned with the dog overpopulation problem have laid the blame at the feet of dog breeders. But there are different kinds of dog breeders; some are taking responsibility for their actions and others aren't. The dog breeder who is striving to produce a better dog, the dog who most closely resembles that breed's standard and is physically, emotionally and genetically healthy, may inadvertently be contributing to the overpopulation problem simply by producing puppies. However, such breeders are to be commended for their efforts to produce better dogs, especially if they have a waiting list of potential owners for each litter, are producing sound, healthy dogs, spay or neuter pet puppies before they leave the premises and are willing to take back any dog who cannot remain in its original home. Many breeders will take back a dog for any reason for the life of the dog. They are certainly not the ones contributing to the problem of homeless, unwanted dogs.

However, the so-called "backyard" breeders—breeders who are breeding a beloved pet but know nothing (or very little) about genetics or the problems faced by their breed—can definitely be contributing to the problem. They may or may not sell their puppies with any kind of a contract and have no facilities to take back unwanted dogs.

Breeding Better Dogs

Pearl, a Shar-Pei, was a pale gold, the color of a cream-colored pearl, for which she had been named. Unfortunately, physically she wasn't a jewel. Her skin looked moth-eaten with numerous red, raw, hairless spots. Several folds of skin looked irritated and Pearl repeatedly tried to chew one on her back. One eye teared incessantly and kept blinking shut. "She has already had two surgeries on her eyes," her owner said, "and I think she'll need another. We've already spent a fortune on her veterinary bills and she's only two years old. But I don't mind spending the money. We'll get it all back when she has puppies."

Unfortunately, this conversation, which really did take place, is replayed all too often. People often breed their dog because it has "papers," mistakenly believing that registration papers imply quality. They do not. Registration papers for a dog are like those for a car; no statement of the dog's (or car's) quality is on the papers. Other people believe a dog is breedable simply because its pedigree contains many champions. Still others, like Pearl's owner, believe their dog should be bred simply because it was expensive to buy.

With the numerous genetic defects found in today's purebred dogs and with the serious dog population problem, only the very best dogs should be bred. That means dogs whose parents, grandparents and great-grandparents have been screened for genetic health defects, and dogs who are excellent physical and emotional representatives of their breed. The dogs should also have the working instincts that their breed was designed to have; herding dogs should be able to herd and bird dogs should be able to point, flush or retrieve.

There should also be serious, responsible homes lined up for all possible puppies before any bitch is bred. A casual, "Oh, yeah, I'd love a pup" is not a serious commitment; a $100 nonrefundable deposit is.

Many animal rights organizations are pressing for a ban on all dog breeding. Stopping all breeding is like throwing the baby out with the bath water. Although we do need less breeding overall, we also need more responsible breeding, breeding that produces better-quality companion animals—companion animals that have good homes.

Dogs that are bred should have the working instincts their breed was designed to possess.

The puppy mills, or puppy farms, that churn out dogs like livestock are definitely contributing to the overpopulation problem. They breed vast numbers of puppies, most of which are sold to pet stores where they are, in turn, sold to buyers with no idea of what they are getting. These dogs may come with a 30-day money-back guarantee, but no one will be looking out for the dog afterwards if it ends up in the hands of irresponsible owners.

Why Are Dogs Relinquished?

Why are so many dogs unwanted? Seattle Purebred Dog Rescue (SPDR) asked owners that very question when they brought their dogs to SPDR. Here's what they found:

82 No time for the dog

66 Moving, didn't want to take dog

29 Moving to a place where dogs aren't allowed

21 Divorce

16 Didn't have room for a dog

13 Dog has bitten people

13 Had too many dogs

13 Owner died

13 Dog was found as a stray

11 Couldn't afford the dog (including vet fees)

10 Owner is ill

10 Complaints from neighbors, including barking

10 Doesn't get along, fights with other dogs

10 Aggressive to other animals; cats, livestock

8 Didn't have a fenced yard

8 "Too much dog"

7 Allergies

7 Didn't like the dog

7 Dogs confiscated, including by police during arrests

6 Destructive, chewing

6 Family has a new baby

6 Owner didn't understand dog's behavior

5 Dog digs

5 Owner travels too much

5 Didn't want a dog

4 Dog was an unwanted gift

4 Unable to care for dog

4 Not house-trained

4	Too rough, jumps up on people	2	Dog is afraid of sounds
3	Owner has new puppy	1	New spouse
3	Didn't make it as a working dog	1	Last of litter
2	Not protective	1	No longer showing the dog
2	Needs training	1	Stud dog was not breeding quality
2	Sheds too much		
2	Dog does not retrieve or hunt	1	No papers; wanted a registered dog for breeding
2	Redecorated, no longer want dog	1	Dog was pregnant
2	Owners bred the bitch, kept a puppy, got rid of mother	1	Dog was ill
		1	Dog "needs" to hunt
		1	Dog was "too much hassle"
2	Child too rough with dog	1	Owner homeless
2	Fleas	1	Owner afraid of dog

So what do these figures say? Well, first of all, they confirm that many dogs are given up for frivolous reasons. To most dog owners, redecorating is certainly not a valid reason for giving up a dog. In fact, many dog owners take their dog into consideration when redecorating, installing carpet that matches the dog hair, instead of the opposite! Commitment to the dog is a necessary part of responsible dog ownership and people who would give up their dog for such frivolous reasons shouldn't own a dog, or any pet.

However, since many of these owners seem to lack the knowledge of how to properly care for a dog, do not seem interested in educating themselves about the dog's behavior and needs and do not try to get the training needed to have a well-behaved pet, perhaps giving their dog up is for the best. Not everyone should own a dog. However, surrendering the dog is for the best only if those owners don't turn around and get another dog, hoping that "this one will be different."

During this SPDR survey, more than 500 people refused to give any answer at all as to why they were relinquishing their dog. Five hundred people gave no answer. Why is that? Were they embarrassed because they were giving the dog up? Had they given up too easily? Many were probably unaware of the time and effort that a dog requires. Perhaps the dog had been an impulse purchase or a gift. Maybe the dog had been for the children, who quickly grew tired of the responsibility.

Changing Those Statistics

Education is the key to successful dog ownership, both before someone gets a dog and after. Potential owners need to learn what dog is right for them and their particular lifestyle; after all, every breed has its own characteristics and each dog is an individual. They need to know how to find that perfect puppy.

Potential dog owners also need to know *before* they buy a dog that dogs require a considerable amount of time, affection and money. They need to know exactly what living with a dog is all about. A dog is not like a car; it can't be parked in the backyard, waiting for you when you happen to have the time.

Dog owners need to learn what makes their dog behave the way it does. When they understand why dogs jump on people, chew on the furniture and dig in the yard, they can then change, solve or learn to live with some of these common canine behaviors instead of getting rid of the dog. Education and training for both the owner and the dog is a necessity.

Where can that education come from? The media is the obvious answer: pet publications, consumer magazines, radio, talk shows and television. Every time there is media coverage of a negative incident with a dog, the reporter could talk to three or four experts and find out what went wrong and why.

Education must come from the community's pet professionals, too. It's easy to set up a seminar at the local humane society to talk about spaying or neutering, grooming, fleas and ticks, vaccinations, house-training, obedience and much, much more.

The Need for Rescue

Responsible dog breeding is a goal for the future that is coming about today. Many breeders are scaling back their operations, striving to produce only the best dogs possible. However, many backyard breeders still haven't heard the message. Also, even though several puppy mills have been closed, there are many still in operation, churning out puppies by the thousands.

Suzanne Kane and HART

Suzanne Kane was the head of the Ventura Water Department when she was approached by an animal control officer who shared Kane's love of animals. The animal control officer drove Kane to a poor area of the city. Inside a dilapidated house was an elderly woman and her black and white dog. "I'm dying," the woman told Kane, "and I have no family. Can you please take care of my dog?"

Saving that dog started Kane on a journey she never expected to take. "I had no intention of starting a rescue organization. But I found out quickly that no one cared about this woman, let alone her dog." The little dog, Babe, went home with Kane, and she and her husband set up an organization called HART (Humane Animal Rescue Team).

HART concentrates primarily on the pets of the terminally ill, victims of violence and the homeless. Since its start in 1984, HART has rescued, neutered and placed over 20,000 companion animals. Through its bimonthly newspaper, *Muttmatchers Messenger,* HART publicizes the stories of numerous pets needing homes, including older or disabled dogs. HART's volunteers worked tirelessly after the California earthquakes in 1994 left many pets homeless.

All of these available puppies, combined with so many dog owners with unrealistic expectations of dog ownership, have created the need for dog rescue. Purebred dog rescue is generally defined as the movement to locate and care for purebred dogs in need, saving as many as possible from euthanasia and placing those dogs in responsible, permanent homes.

Purebred dog rescue groups are working all over the country and range in size from one-person operations that save one dog at a time to vast operations run by national breed clubs. Some of the groups, like Seattle Purebred Dog Rescue, attempt to rescue as many dogs as possible of many different breeds. Other groups, especially those run by breed clubs, only rescue dogs of their particular breed.

To find out more about this organization, contact HART, P.O. Box 920, Fillmore, CA 93016 (805) 524-4542.

Dogs can also be victims of death, violence and homelessness.

Because there is no governing agency for rescue groups, there are no concrete figures available on how many dogs are saved each year. However, each group keeps its own records and the numbers can be staggering. For example, the Golden Retriever Club of San Diego County Rescue Service has been saving Golden Retrievers since 1980 and, as of this writing, has placed close to 1,000 dogs in new, permanent homes.

Nationally, the average shelter places only 10 percent of the dogs brought in by their owners, not including strays or abandoned animals. Clearly, rescue groups can serve an enormous need in caring for the 90 percent of dogs who are not lucky enough to find a new home right away. In fact, many shelters and rescue groups work hand in hand, with the shelters maintaining a list of telephone numbers and contacts for each breed and calling on specific rescue groups when a dog of their breed is brought in.

CHAPTER 2

• •

What Is Purebred Dog Rescue?

Purebred dog rescue groups grew out of the need to find homes for purebred dogs. Although many people think the only dogs found in shelters and humane societies are mixed breeds, the opposite is true. Thousands of purebred dogs can be found in shelters all over the country on any given day. By organizing volunteers, networking with various pet professionals and educating the public, rescue groups hope to place unwanted purebred dogs in new, permanent, suitable homes. Their hope is that by doing so, the number of purebred dogs euthanized or living out their lives in shelters will be decreased.

How Is Rescue Different from Shelter Adoption?

Dogs available for adoption in a shelter situation may or may not have any known history. The dog may have been a stray or he may have been given up by its owners with little information offered. Many shelters, concerned about privacy laws and potential lawsuits, share very little information with potential adopters, even when information about the dog is available.

While rescue groups do take dogs of their breed out of shelters, they also get many dogs directly from their owners and in other circumstances (such as police raids) where the dog's history is known. If the dog is given to the rescue group by its owner, most groups require the owner to complete a questionnaire that asks about the dog's health, behavior and training. Seattle Purebred Dog Rescue asks the following questions:

> Is the dog house trained? Crate trained? Paper trained?
>
> Where did you originally get the dog?
>
> Are shots up to date?
>
> Is the dog spayed or neutered?
>
> Do you have health records that you can give the new owner?
>
> Does the dog have any health problems? Allergies?
>
> Has the dog been to an obedience class?
>
> List the dog's commands, tricks or skills.
>
> What brand of food does the dog eat?
>
> How is the dog around other dogs? Cats? Kids?
>
> Does the dog have any behavior problems?

Additional questions ask about the dog's most appealing traits, its biggest problems and much more. When this much information is available, people considering adopting the dog can make a more knowledgeable decision. How much training will the dog need and can you do it? Are you willing to house train the dog? Do you have other pets that the dog will need to get along with? Even knowing what food the dog is used to eating can make life easier, since the stress of an abrupt change of food will not be added to all the other stresses on a dog who is changing homes.

Rescue groups also screen the dogs they accept for potentially dangerous situations. Aggressive dogs, or dogs that are known biters, are rarely (if ever) accepted into rescue programs. In comparison, the unknown history of some shelter dogs makes it difficult to screen for potentially dangerous dogs. Aussie Rescue &

Placement Helpline, a rescue organization sanctioned by the Australian Shepherd Club of America, has strict guidelines regarding behavior. No dog will be accepted into the program if it has any history of growling, snapping, nipping or biting. If, while the dog is in foster care, it shows aggressive behavior, it will be euthanized. While this might seem rather harsh, it is necessary. A potentially dangerous dog cannot be placed in a home where it could cause harm. Moral, ethical and legal issues must prevail.

Some rescue groups also take dogs that would be considered unadoptable by most shelters. Yankee Golden Retriever Rescue will accept senior Golden Retrievers (eight years and older), many of whom have special veterinary needs simply because they're older. YGRR will also accept Goldens with other special medical needs and have helped dogs with epilepsy, vision problems, hearing loss and missing limbs. In most shelters, these dogs would be considered unadoptable and would have been euthanized soon after they arrived.

Most rescue groups deal with one specific breed and have volunteers who are very knowledgeable about that breed. Groups that deal with more than one breed usually maintain a list of breed representatives—volunteers with experience and knowledge about one or two particular breeds. Dog owners considering giving up their dog can talk to these experts, who understand the breed. Sometimes after learning more about their dog and its breed, or after getting some help, these owners decide to keep their dog.

Potential adopters can also talk to these experts, ask questions about the breed and get honest answers. What is this breed really like? How active is it? How much exercise does it require? How much does the breed shed? How much grooming does it need? What should a new owner expect from this breed? With answers to these and other questions, a potential adopter can make a more informed decision.

Unlike shelters, where dogs are kept in kennels and busy staff may have limited time to interact with them, many rescue groups use a network of foster homes to care for homeless dogs until the right adoptive home is available. The foster homes give dogs a chance to settle down and live in a more normal situation. The foster owners can evaluate the dogs' behavior, assist with training and can get to know the dogs. Potential new owners can then have a realistic assessment of who the dog is and what it is really like.

Greyhound Pets of America uses a network of temporary homes to foster each rescued retired racing Greyhound. The foster owners get to know each dog and can then provide useful information, such as, "This dog chases cats and shows strong prey drive and should be placed in a home without small pets," or "That dog loves all other pets, is great with people of all ages and particularly likes small children." This information can help in placing the dog in the right new home.

With experienced volunteers, rescue groups can also help with the adoption process. Potential new owners can be matched with a dog that will best suit their needs and lifestyles; counseling can be provided to help the dog and owner through the transition; and information about veterinarians, grooming and training can be available.

All of the reputable rescue groups screen potential new owners carefully. Many require a home visit so that the group can verify that the dog is going to a home and not to a research lab. Many groups also require that the new owner's yard be securely fenced, that the dog live in the house and not the yard and that other dogs in the family be dog friendly. Some rescue groups also require personal references. (Chapter 4 will discuss the adoption process in more detail.)

Several rescue groups stress dog owner education as one of their primary goals. Potential new dog owners need to know what owning a dog is all about; that dogs require love and affection, time, money and a 12- to 14-year commitment. Although dogs can be wonderful friends and companions, potential dog owners need to know the negative side of ownership, too: grooming the dog, picking up feces, vacuuming the carpet and treating the house and yard for fleas. Emergency veterinary bills can be expensive, as can routine shots, worming and unexpected illnesses or injuries.

People also need to know what a particular breed is like before they buy or adopt a dog. The Aussie Rescue & Placement Helpline has compiled information about Australian Shepherds given up by their owners and has found that most Aussies are given up because owners don't really understand some basic characteristics of the breed. First, Aussies are very smart dogs and, if not trained, will out-smart their owners. Aussies are active dogs and need daily exercise and an outlet for their energy. Aussies are very protective and require training and guidance to channel this effectively. Aussies are not good backyard dogs and need to be with their people as much as possible. When the breed's needs are not met, the dogs can be destructive or they can develop other behavior problems such as barking or escaping from the yard.

All breeds have their own unique characteristics and needs and potential dog owners need to know what to expect of and from their breed. It is far better that they know what to expect so that they can learn how to work with the dog, than to find out later and get rid of the dog.

Purebred Dog Rescue Groups

There are hundreds of rescue groups all over the country. Some rescue any dog in need, regardless of breed heritage, age or circumstances. Other groups rescue only purebred dogs and some rescue only one specific breed. One thing all of these groups have in common is a desire to save dogs. Some of the groups can save large numbers of dogs; others rescue one dog at a time.

It would be impossible to describe here all of the groups doing this work. However, I do want to highlight a few groups to show how some of the organizations work. Each has a similar goal, but their approach to that goal might be slightly different. Throughout this book, profiles will highlight other groups, their work and some of their accomplishments. There are hundreds of rescue groups across the nation, and there just isn't enough space in this book to list them all. There are many, many wonderful rescue groups and hard-working volunteers doing great work for dogs.

Seattle Purebred Dog Rescue was founded in 1987 and is an all volunteer, non-profit organization dedicated to placing pure-bred dogs into carefully screened new homes. The goal of SPDR is to offer dog owners an alternative to taking an unwanted pure-bred dog to the shelter. Working as an adoption referral service by networking with the local dog fancy, dogs can be found new homes and as a result, area shelters can lower their euthanasia rates.

SPDR maintains a listing of breed experts who screen the dogs offered to the group. These experts can spot potential behavior problems that might eliminate the dog from the program (such as aggressive behavior towards people). The experts can also provide breed-specific information to owners thinking of giving up their dog, or to potential adopters who need more specific breed information.

In its first years of operation, SPDR placed between 200 and 300 dogs a year. In 1995, more than 3,000 dogs came into SPDR's program.

Yankee Golden Retriever Rescue, Inc. was established in 1985 by Joan Puglia and Susan Foster. These two women were disturbed by the increasing numbers of Goldens being found in local shelters and decided to do something about it. Based in Massachusetts, Yankee Golden Retriever Rescue employs one part-time employee; all the other work is done by volunteers. Recognized by the Internal Revenue Service as a charity, Yankee relies on donations, membership dues and fund-raising events for its income.

Along with hundreds of healthy, young Goldens, many Goldens of advanced age and many with special needs are helped, too. Yankee Golden Retriever Rescue placed its 2,000th Golden Retriever into a new home in 1996, a notable achievement.

The All Breed Rescue Alliance (ABRA) is a working alliance whose members represent a number of different breed rescue groups in the Mid-Atlantic region. ABRA's primary goal is to ensure that more unwanted pets can find responsible, permanent homes. The group publishes an annual directory that lists the ABRA breed representatives, adoption procedures and a description of specific breed characteristics. The group also sponsors an annual fair that features ABRA members, rescue dogs and information about specific breeds. Other activities are scheduled to inform the public not just about rescue, but also about responsible pet ownership.

ABRA has also put together a how-to booklet for other rescue groups titled *How to Start a Rescue,* with information about networking, publicity, evaluating dogs and evaluating potential new owners. Copies of blank forms for evaluations, adoption contracts and follow-up visits are also included. You can write to ABRA at 357 Third Avenue, Phoenixville, PA 19460.

Collie Humane Care is a New York State, not-for-profit group organized to provide a rescue and adoption program for Collies. All Collies go into foster care until new homes are found. Experts can provide educational materials for Collie owners, or potential owners, and their children. The group also has a dog training program so that new Collie owners can train their dogs, learn responsible dog ownership and overcome any behavior problems their dog may have.

AKC National, Regional and Local Breed Clubs are groups of people interested in one specific breed. The American Kennel Club (AKC) recognizes a parent breed club for each of the breeds it registers. This parent club governs or supervises many of the activities within the breed, including rescue efforts. Most breed club members show their dogs in Conformation, Obedience or performance events. Many are also breeders.

Some parent clubs, such as the Papillon Club of America, have organized rescue efforts at the national level. Other clubs have placed rescue work in the hands of their local clubs or chapters. The AKC's monthly magazine, the *AKC Gazette,* maintains a listing of club rescue programs that is published every November. For the most recent list, call the AKC Library at (212) 696-8246 or visit the AKC's Website at http://www.akc.org.

Irish Wolfhound Rescue rescues and places approximately 25 to 40 Irish Wolfhounds per year in an area covering the far west, including California, Nevada, Utah, Arizona and New Mexico. The group is constantly networking with veterinarians, humane societies, shelters and other pet professionals. With this network in place, if an Irish Wolfhound is turned in to a shelter or if a veterinarian hears a client say she can no longer keep her dog, a rescue volunteer is contacted.

Cassie Gets a Job

Cassie was rescued by the Houston, Texas, Humane Society. An animal control officer picked up Cassie and four other dogs from their former owner's backyard. Their owner had been evicted and had simply left the dogs alone in the yard. The Humane Society called the Aussie Rescue & Placement Helpline.

Cassie stayed with a foster home volunteer and started obedience training. She learned commands quickly and seemed to be eager to learn. Another volunteer called Cassie's foster owner, asking if a rescue dog was available who showed potential to be trained as a service dog for a woman, Joanne Dixon, who has multiple sclerosis. Cassie's foster owner volunteered Cassie, and Dixon was invited to meet the dog. There was an immediate bond between the two.

Cassie stayed with her foster owner for several more weeks so that she could learn to back up, wait, walk next to a cane and a walker, wear a backpack and more. When delivered to Dixon, Cassie settled into her new home quietly and with assurance. At

The group maintains a list of screened and approved new homes so that as a dog becomes available, a home is ready and waiting. If there is a question about a dog's temperament, or if the dog needs veterinary care or is awaiting surgery, foster homes will keep the dog until it is ready for adoption. The trust also provides after-adoption follow-up counseling and is available to answer questions and provide referrals to obedience trainers and other needed services. The group maintains a personal connection with each adopted Irish Wolfhound and its new family, sending out New Year's cards, birthday cards, reminders of vaccinations due and thank-you cards for donations.

The Aussie Rescue & Placement Helpline is a recognized committee under the auspices of the Australian Shepherd Club of America. This group has volunteers all over the country who work

this writing, her training is continuing with the goal of having her certified as a service dog in the near future.

To find out more about this organization, contact ARPH, P.O. Box 732, Leona Valley, CA 93551 (800) 892-ASCA.

Cassie found new life as a service dog.

Tink the Athlete

Carly glanced at her alarm clock as the telephone rang. "Six A.M.! Geez!" she muttered as she answered the phone, "Hello?"

"Is this Papillon rescue?"

"Yes it is."

"My mother passed away yesterday and I can't keep her dog. Can you take it?"

That afternoon a green station wagon pulled up to Carly's house and Tink officially became the ward of Southern California Papillon Rescue. A handsome tricolored Papillon, he was obviously confused about his situation and spent most of his time trying to climb into Carly's lap. However, she was used to shell-shocked little dogs and was infinitely patient with him. It took a few weeks, but eventually the little dog's bubbling personality started to show.

When a young woman called asking about a Papillon who might do well in dog sports, Carly immediately thought of Tink and asked the woman to come over. Sandy and Tink hit it off right away and three days later he moved to his new, permanent home.

When Tink earned his Companion Dog Obedience title, Sandy sent Carly a copy of it. When he earned his Companion Dog Excellent, Utility Dog and Tracking Dog titles she did the same thing. Later, when he earned his Agility title, Carly framed her copy of that, too. And later, as his muzzle started to gray, Tink was certified as a Therapy Dog and Sandy sent Carly a copy of that certificate, too.

to rescue and place Australian Shepherds. The program runs on the dedication and love that members have for their breed; in fact, as with many other rescue groups, all of the workers are volunteers and receive no compensation for their hard work. Payment is the sense of accomplishment they get when an Aussie is placed into a loving, caring and permanent home. The Helpline also provides information on the unique temperament,

When Tink passed away at the age of 15, Sandy and Carly met for coffee and talked about the spunky little dog, his accomplishments and the joy he brought to so many lives. As Sandy hugged Carly and started to walk away, she turned back to Carly and asked, "Oh, by the way, do you know of a rescue Papillon that might enjoy dog sports?"

Tink proved to be a huge sports fan.

intelligence, exercise needs and training requirements of the breed. Each issue of the *Aussie Times,* the club's magazine, profiles some of the dogs who need homes (as do many breed club magazines).

Seattle Purebred Dog Rescue is a large organization. But some rescue groups are quite small. However, small groups can do good work, too, even rescuing one dog at a time.

Kathy Sullivan rescues Pomeranians. Her local club doesn't have a rescue group but Kathy had seen Poms in the local shelter and felt that there was a need. Unable to convince anyone else to help her, she started taking in one dog at a time. "I make sure each dog is spayed or neutered, vaccinated and house-trained. Then I match the dog's personality to someone on my waiting list to adopt a Pom. When that dog is placed, then I am free to rescue another." In the past four years, she has placed 17 dogs.

The Rio Grande Valley Golden Retriever Club is a small group that has placed over 300 Goldens since the group began in 1983. Each dog's placement in a new, responsible, permanent home is an accomplishment in itself.

Terry Sagnon has been rescuing Papillons for over 10 years. She works by herself, making sure the local animal shelters and veterinarians have her number. "Luckily for me and for the breed, Papillons have small litters and are usually in great demand," she said. "I usually get calls from people whose elderly relative has passed away, leaving behind a distraught Papillon." Sagnon fosters the dogs in her own home with her three resident Paps. By watching them in a home setting, she feels she can better evaluate their training, behavior and personality.

When asked why she does this work, she said, "When I pick up a Papillon, especially from a home where an owner has passed away, the dog is emotionally crushed and literally feels lost. When I foster that dog, teaching it to enjoy life again and then place it in another loving, caring home, I know that the work I am doing is worthwhile. Then, when I come back for a check-up visit and see that dog bonded to its new owners, happy and joyful as only a Papillon can be, well, there is no feeling like it."

Rescue has its downsides, too, though. Many volunteers get depressed and angry at the dog-owning public after processing dog after dog after dog. Some of the dogs are neglected, some are abused, many lack veterinary care, most lack grooming and almost all lack training. When the shelters are full of dogs needing homes and the classified ads in the newspaper list litter after litter of purebred dogs, trying to make a difference can be very depressing. Volunteers can feel overwhelmed.

Sometimes, too, a placement will not work. A carefully screened home and a thoroughly evaluated dog may not mesh well. Perhaps there is a personality conflict. Sometimes an unknown side of the dog's temperament surfaces. Maybe the adoptive owner was not honest with the volunteer. There are many reasons. Sometimes when a home doesn't work, the dog will simply come back to the rescue group. Unfortunately, if the dog has bitten or has been traumatized by the process, the dog may be euthanized.

Certainly, rescuing a needy dog can be its own reward. But why do volunteers go through all of this unending work and emotional trauma? Billie Stewart of Wayeh Kennels, a member of the Alaskan Malamute Protection League in Kentucky, explained it best: "When I was younger I did a lot of backpacking. An important part of the backpacker's code was to carry out more than you brought in; picking up trash that other people would leave behind. As a Malamute breeder, I know that I, too, can make mistakes. It's entirely possible that a dog I bred could end up in a shelter somewhere without me knowing about it. I feel compelled to follow the same code as I did as a backpacker; I want to carry out more than I bring in. As long as I can, I will try to breed responsibly and will do what I can to pick up after the mistakes of others."

What Does the Future Look Like?

When discussing the future, most rescue groups mention three things—a lack of money, the never-ending supply of dogs needing help and the unrealistic expectations or lack of commitment of dog owners.

When asked what problems their group faces in the future, Gerry McGee, media representative for Greyhound Pets of America, said, "Money, money, money, money! This is probably the unifying cry of all animal rescue groups. We have many fund-raisers during the year to help defray some of our expenses."

In order to have the funds needed to pay veterinary fees and other costs, Yankee Golden Retriever Rescue has a mail-order catalog of Golden Retriever specialty items and a calendar featuring adopted Golden Retrievers. The group also holds an annual silent, fund-raising auction. In the future, Yankee hopes to raise enough money to build its own shelter and training facility.

Many breed clubs raise money for their rescue groups in similar ways, donating the proceeds of dog shows, raffles and sales to rescue. Unfortunately, the need for funds keeps growing because there is a seemingly unending supply of dogs needing responsible, permanent homes. So what can be done about this unending supply of dogs?

Almost all of the rescue groups I interviewed for this book require that dogs be spayed or neutered prior to adoption (unlike most shelters, which simply suggest it). The others had a contract with the new owner that required the dog to be spayed or neutered after adoption.

Spay and neuter programs do work to cut down on the numbers of dogs facing euthanasia. The Animal Foundation International's low-cost spay and neuter clinic opened in Las Vegas in 1989, and 12,000 sterilizations have been performed each year. The cost of animal control, the numbers of rescues and the total number of animals euthanized in the region have all dropped significantly.

Early age spaying and neutering have been endorsed by both the American Kennel Club and the American Veterinary Medical Association (AVMA). "The AVMA supports the concept of early (eight to 16 weeks of age) ovariohysterectomies and gonadectomies in dogs and cats in an effort to stem the overpopulation problems in these species," says the AVMA's policy statement. The AKC says, in part, "The AKC encourages breeders to breed only for the improvement of the breed and only when the produce of the breeding can be assured proper homes and care. The AKC recommends that breeders encourage puppy purchasers to have their puppies spayed or neutered to prevent accidental breeding and to

Questions About Spaying and Neutering

What does spay or neuter mean?

Spay means the surgical removal of the ovaries and uterus of a female dog. This eliminates any further reproductive cycles or seasons, and the female dog cannot reproduce.

Neutering means the surgical removal of a male dog's testicles, called castration. The male dog then can no longer reproduce.

Why should my dog be spayed or neutered?

Because over 21 million companion animals are killed in the United States in a single year! These animals were born into a world where there simply are not enough caring, responsible homes for them.

Is this surgery harmful to my dog?

Spaying and neutering dogs removes the organs that produce sexual hormones. This can have a calming effect on the dogs and takes away the urge to reproduce, eliminating the male dog's desire to escape from the yard, fight and roam.

Spaying and neutering also reduces the chance of cancers later in life by almost 80 percent.

But don't spayed and neutered dogs get fat?

Dogs gain weight much like people do. When a person or dog eats too much and gets too little exercise, the body will gain weight. An active dog fed a healthy diet will not get fat.

Is it true that my female dog should have a litter of puppies before she's spayed?

That's an old wives' tale and is entirely false.

What if I don't want to DO that to my male dog?

Dogs don't make love; they reproduce. A male dog doesn't know what he's missing and does not mope about it. He doesn't get depressed. Instead, he will live a longer, healthy, safer life after he's been neutered!

Isn't is wonderful for my kids to see the miracle of life?

Prenatal care for the mother dog and veterinary care for the puppies can be expensive. Are you prepared for that? Are you also going to share with your children the tragedy of death when some of the puppies don't make it? What about when you have several four- or five-month-old puppies that you can't find homes for? Will you just drop them off at the humane society?

Remember, responsible breeders breed only for the good of the breed and take responsibility for every dog they breed for the life of the dog. Are you ready to take on that responsibility? With so many unwanted and unneeded puppies being born, this is no excuse for a litter.

avoid breeding merely to produce puppies." (For more on this issue, see "The Case for Early Spay and Neuter" by Darlene Arden in the September 1994 *AKC Gazette.*)

Education, of both owners and breeders, can also help, and most rescue groups either have educational programs already in place or are formulating them.

Many of the dogs turned in to rescue have been produced by breeders. Some of those breeders were so-called "backyard" or amateur breeders. Others were reputable show dog breeders. As many rescue groups have pointed out, all breeders need to be responsible.

Responsible breeding begins by acknowledging that not all dogs should be bred; in fact, very few should be. Only the best when compared to the breed standard (taking into account physical conformation, genetic health, temperament and working ability) should even be considered for breeding. Then, a breeding should be considered only when more than enough potential new homes are available and deposits have been made for future puppies.

Responsible breeders also need to sell pet puppies on spay/neuter contracts or have the surgeries performed before selling the young dogs. Many veterinarians will now perform spays and neuters at a very young age and research has shown that there has been little to no harm in doing the surgery as early as eight to 10 weeks of age.

Responsible breeders must also make sure that potential puppy buyers have realistic expectations about what to expect from their breed. Don't sugarcoat the breed; instead, tell potential puppy buyers what the breed is really like. How much exercise does the breed need? How much grooming? Is the breed easily trained? Or are the dogs of your breed normally independent and stubborn?

Nick Davis, a long-time Australian Shepherd breeder, warns potential buyers that his dogs are working dogs and do not make good pets. Davis says his dogs are more active than many other Aussies and are quite intense. "My dogs need to work and I tell people that. I would rather scare away buyers than have someone buy one of my dogs and be unhappy, or worse yet, mistreat or ruin one of my dogs," he said.

Responsible breeders also need to stay in touch with puppy buyers. This way, if problems do come up the breeders can offer advice and potential solutions. If a puppy (or adult dog) can no longer remain in its original home, the breeder must be willing to take back the dog. Responsible breeders are responsible for all the dogs they breed, for as long as those dogs are alive.

Unfortunately, a very large number of dogs are not bred by breeders at all, but instead are raised like livestock in puppy mills or farms—commercial operations that breed dogs and produce puppies for pet shops to sell. Commercial sales of puppies is big business. Millions of dollars each year are made by the farmers, the wholesalers and the pet stores.

Although some puppy farms do try to treat their dogs well, others do not and in fact, treat their dogs horribly. The dogs normally live in cages with wire floors so that urine and feces fall through to the ground or onto the dogs in the cages stacked below. Many times there will be two to three dogs per cage. Rarely are the dogs taken out of the cages and in fact, many dogs rescued from puppy mills have no idea what grass is. The dogs receive no human contact except at feeding times.

There is no thought given to breeding the best dogs of each breed, nor is there genetic testing for hereditary defects. Dogs are bred to satisfy the demand for popular or rare breeds at pet shops all over the country. Potential buyers are not given any screening to make sure they're ready for the responsibility of owning a dog or that they're aware of the dog's physical and emotional needs. And while many pet shops offer a 30- or 90-day money back guarantee, they do not assume any responsibility for the long-term welfare of the dogs they sell.

Rescue groups have to deal with the fallout of puppy mills. Dog owners who bought a cute puppy at a pet store on an impulse are disillusioned when the puppy is shedding all over the house, is chewing up the furniture or has outgrown the apartment. The dog either ends up at a local shelter or with the rescue group.

When a puppy mill is shut down by local animal control authorities, the rescue groups are called in to deal with the unfortunate dogs housed there, too. Over and over again, rescue groups for Akitas, Cocker Spaniels, Papillons, Shih Tzu and other breeds have had to make decisions as to the future (or lack of) for dozens and dozens of dogs. During most rescue operations, some dogs can be saved, especially young dogs. But many dogs have to be destroyed because of health problems or lack of socialization to people.

Karen Tiburg, a rescue volunteer for German Shepherds, said, "A German Shepherd Dog that has been caged for many years and has had no socialization to people can be a dangerous animal. As much as I love the breed, I understand that many of the dogs I try to rescue from puppy mills must be destroyed. The only way I can continue my work is that I know I am saving these intelligent dogs from further suffering."

John Savoy, a volunteer for Shih Tzu rescue, said about puppy mills, "Dog fanciers must spread the word in their own communities that most puppies found in pet shops come from puppy mills. If there were no demand for puppies, pet stores would stop selling them. More and more pet stores all over the country, have stopped selling puppies because of local efforts by concerned dog owners. But the war is not yet won; as long as puppy mills exist, it will be an on-going battle."

Lyn Bingham, a director for Seattle Purebred Dog Rescue, said, "Purebred dog rescue is one of the most rewarding aspects of the human-dog relationship. There is no fame or fortune in dog rescue; it is something we do for no other reason than to attempt to give these dogs a second chance at life."

PART II

Adopting a Purebred Rescue Dog

CHAPTER 3

•••

Choose a Rescue Dog for the Right Reasons

The decision to add a dog to your life is not one to be made lightly or on impulse. You must first evaluate your needs, the needs of your family, what you want in a dog and whether the breeds you're considering will make a good match. Purchasing or adopting a dog—any dog—is a long-term commitment; with proper care, many dogs can live 12 to 15 years. Before you make any decision, make sure you know exactly how a dog will affect your life.

Questions to Ask Yourself

What do you want to do with a dog? Do you want an athletic dog that can go jogging with you? Do you want to participate in dog sports? Do you want to use a dog for its native abilities, such as tracking, hunting, sledding or herding? Do you want a protective dog? Do you want a dog to snuggle with in the evenings? Do you want a people-oriented dog that will be your shadow, or do you like more independent dogs?

How much time can you devote to the dog? Dogs require a substantial time commitment from you. A dog will need to spend time with you; after all, you are getting a dog for companionship, aren't you? And that takes time to develop and nurture. Your dog will also require grooming, training, play times and exercise. All of these things take time.

A Noble Duchess

Diane Reppy, a volunteer working for German Shepherd Rescue Inc. in Pennsylvania, received a call from a shelter in Maryland about a three-month-old puppy that had been dropped off with them, supposedly because the puppy had severe hip dysplasia. After several conversations with the shelter, the shelter agreed to pay for half of the surgical costs to correct the dysplasia, while German Shepherd Rescue would pay the other half. This was a tremendous donation on the shelter's part.

After many more telephone calls, Reppy was able to find a volunteer who could pick up the puppy in Rockville, Maryland, and take it as far as Baltimore. Another volunteer met the puppy in Baltimore and took it as far as Lansdale, where she spent the night. The next day found the puppy traveling to Quakerstown and finally to the veterinarian who vaccinated and spayed her. The next step was her hip surgery, which was performed at the Malvern, Pennsylvania, Veterinary Orthopedic Center.

Does everyone want a new dog? If some of the family members are less than pleased at the prospect of adding a dog, the dog will suffer for it. One person's animosity, lack of caring, anger, neglect or abuse could severely traumatize the dog. Everyone must agree to adopt a dog.

Will a dog fit in with your present living arrangements? Dogs take up physical space, and if you live in a tiny studio apartment a Saint Bernard might take up more room than you are willing or able to give up. Apartment dwellers will also want to avoid breeds known to be barkers. Also, do you need permission from your landlord before adopting a dog? Does your rental contract or lease allow dogs? Are there size limits? If you own your home, does your homeowners association have any limits on dogs?

As the puppy was recuperating from her surgery, a couple from Macungie called. They had just lost their old German Shepherd and were looking for another. They drove to see the puppy and promptly fell in love with Duchess.

Duchess had to wait a few more weeks before going to her new home, but soon received permission from the veterinarian as long as her new owners continued her physical therapy. Glad to do so, her new family drove her an hour away from home several times a week for more than two months so that she could continue her swimming therapy at a rehabilitation center for animals.

Reppy said, "At a recent meeting of the rescue group, we all smiled as we passed around the photographs showing a beautiful, mature, noble German Shepherd, Duchess, with her loving family. A happy ending. This is why we do rescue."

To find out more about this organization, contact German Shepherd Rescue Inc., P.O. Box 117, New Ringgold, PA 17960.

How much do you value your interior decorations? If you like an immaculate, pristine house, perhaps you should consider a ceramic dog because dogs can, and do, make a mess. Dogs shed, especially in the spring and fall, although some breeds are worse than others. Dogs track in dirt from outside and carry in leaves, pinecones and other interesting things they wish to share with you. Dogs' tails have been known to clear the coffee table in one sweep. It's amazing how powerful a tail can be!

Is your yard securely fenced? Some breeds are known to be escape artists, especially if left alone for any period of time. Is your yard big enough for a Greyhound to run around and exercise, or is it better suited to a Pomeranian? Is your yard nicely landscaped? Would it bother you if the dog tried to dig up the resident gopher? Some breeds are more prone to digging than others.

Is your yard secure enough for a big dog?

Do you like exercise? All dogs need exercise, but some need more than others. If you dis-like longwalks, hate bicycle riding and don't jog, consider a breed that doesn't need as much exercise. If you like to jog or ride your bicycle, love to throw a Frisbee or tennis ball and enjoy time outside, then get a dog with higher exercise needs.

Can you train this dog? Some breeds are known to be more receptive to training than others. Training requires time, consistency and patience from you as well as the financial outlay for lessons. Keep in mind that the dog who dislikes training the most, the one who will defy or challenge you, is probably the dog who needs it the most!

Can you groom the dog? You will also need to schedule time for grooming. Every dog needs to be groomed regularly. Obviously, a long-coated breed like the Old English Sheepdog requires more grooming time and effort than does a short-haired breed like the Pointer. But all dogs, short-, medium- or long-haired, need to have regular grooming, including having their ears cleaned and toenails trimmed and checking for fleas and ticks.

Do you have even more time? Small things that need to be done daily take time, too. Dogs must be walked, and their feces need to be picked up and disposed of several times every day. The dog's water needs to be changed daily and, of course, the dog must be fed. Play is important for all dogs and time must be allotted for that, as well as for exercise and training.

Can you guess your future? Where do you see yourself in five years? Ten years? Are you climbing the corporate ladder and facing possible transfers? A dog requires a 10- to 15-year commitment. If there is any doubt in your mind about whether you will be able to keep this dog for its entire life, then think again *before* adopting it.

Your Special Dog

Do you have memories of a Shetland Sheepdog that washed away your tears when you were a child? Perhaps you were impressed by the skill and dedication of a German Shepherd Dog guiding its blind master. You can take those personal preferences into consideration when choosing a dog. However, don't build the pedestal too high. Although there are similarities between dogs of a particular breed, each dog is an individual and how any one dog has been raised and trained will have a great effect on what that dog is like as an adult.

Other personal preferences come into play when choosing the right breed and dog for you. Some people love to cuddle a shaggy dog and don't care about the upkeep it requires, while other people enjoy the sleek look of a short-coated dog. Some people like the snub-nosed appearance of a Pug or Bulldog, while other people treasure the longer muzzle of a Greyhound or Collie. All of these things should be taken into consideration.

Evaluating Your Temperament

These questions are not the only ones you should ask yourself as you decide whether or not you're ready for a dog, but they can serve as a guide to help you think about owning a dog and what type of dog might best suit you.

1. When you come home from work you are:

    A. Tired and just want to relax; you spend the evening reading or watching television.

    B. Tired but like to get outside, walking or riding your bicycle.

    C. Glad to get home, can't wait to do something.

    If you answered A, you should either consider a calm, older dog or a ceramic dog. If you answered B, a calm, younger adult dog might suit you. If you answered C, an active young dog should please you.

2. Being the center of a dog's world can be thrilling to some people and overwhelming to others. Do you:

    A. Like being the center of someone's attention?

    B. Like the idea of a dog who follows your every move?

    C. Prefer a dog who is more independent?

    D. Detest being watched or followed? Do you dislike being touched?

    If you answered "yes" to A or B, many breeds will suit your needs, especially the herding and working dogs. If you answered

C, think about some of the hounds or terriers. If you answered D, get a ceramic dog.

3. What is your life like?

    A. Are you retired and live alone?

    B. Do you work and live alone or with one other adult?

    C. Are there active children in the household?

    D. Do you have some health problems that might affect your life with a dog?

    If you answered "yes" to A, you might want to have a dog that is active and entertaining. However, if both A and D describe you, you might need to strike a better balance between a dog that is entertaining but not too physically demanding.

    If you answered "yes" to B, you may need a breed or personality that can stay home alone while you're both at work, or you may want to get a cat instead. If you answered C, you may wish to get a calm medium or large dog that can handle the stimulation of the kids.

There are lots of different breeds. It has been said many times that a dog is not just a dog. There are more than 400 different breeds known worldwide. The differences between many of these breeds is immense. Just compare the Great Dane and the Chihuahua!

Each breed also has its own body type. Each breed's national (or international) club has written a description of the ideal dog, called the breed standard. This description details exactly what the dogs of that breed should look like, from body shape and size to coat length and color, head shape, ear set and even personality and character. This standard is what keeps a Greyhound looking like a Greyhound instead of a Rottweiler.

Every breed of dog was "designed" or bred for a specific purpose. Keep that purpose in mind as you research breeds because that original occupation still has bearing on the breed today and might not fit into what you need (or want) from a dog. For example, herding dogs are usually fairly active dogs that can be taught to herd you, your kids or the family cats. Herding dogs also like to run circles around people, gathering them together as they would sheep. Dogs that hunt by scent, such as Beagles, Basset Hounds and Bloodhounds, would be happiest if they could live with their nose to the ground. Dogs that hunt by sight, such as Whippets, love to chase moving objects, and that could include the family cat.

When you are trying to decide what breed might be best for you, don't be afraid to ask questions. Call your local dog trainer, groomer and veterinarian to find out their opinion of the breeds you're considering. Does this breed seem to be healthy? Does it cause trouble for the groomer? Is it easily trained? What do they think of the breed as a whole?

You also need to consider which sex you want. There are some very different behavior characteristics associated with males and females, especially in certain breeds. Female dogs (called bitches) are usually easier to train than males, especially intact males (dogs that haven't been neutered). Depending upon the breed, females can be very protective, yet less aggressive. Bitches are less prone to fighting than males; however, when two bitches do fight, it is usually a more vicious fight than one between males.

Although the owners of some dogs will debate it, male dogs, especially neutered males, have a tendency to be more affectionate. As a general rule, intact males are more active than females and are more likely to try and escape from the yard and roam. Intact males will also tend to "forget" house-training rules to mark territory. However, most, if not all, rescued dogs (male and female) will either be neutered or spayed upon adoption.

Why Adopt a Rescue Dog?

Many people who have adopted a rescue dog felt they didn't have the time to devote to a puppy or simply didn't want the hassle.

Puppies are a lot of work, especially when they are young, and many people would rather skip the crying, whining, chewing and house-training that comes with a very young puppy.

Other people aren't in a position to cope with a puppy, either emotionally or physically. Susan Baxter wanted a dog for companionship and protection, since her husband is in the military and is often gone for months at a time. However, with their new baby just starting to walk, she felt that coping with a baby and a puppy would be too much. She adopted Rudy, a two-year-old Australian Shepherd whose military owner had been transferred overseas. "I feel a bond with Rudy because my husband is overseas, too, just like his former owner is," she said. "Rudy has been very well trained and although his owners didn't have any kids, he is very gentle and patient with my daughter. He has settled in very well and I'm enjoying his company." She has also kept in touch with Rudy's former owners, sending them pictures of the dog in his new home.

Puppies do require a certain amount of physical dexterity, too, if for nothing else than to catch, groom or clean up after them. Many people with physical disabilities, or the elderly, find it difficult to keep up with a puppy.

Conrad Holmes lost his wife to cancer after 45 years of marriage and the 84-year-old gentleman soon found himself very lonely. He wanted a dog for companionship but decided a puppy was out of the question since his arthritis made it very difficult to bend over. "There is no way I can bend over fast enough to grab a puppy, to take something out of its mouth or even to pick it up. I'd have a heck of a time cleaning messes off the floor." He adopted Gretchen, a retired and rescued racing Greyhound, and has no need to bend over. "Gretchen is perfectly house-trained, doesn't chew on anything and has perfect house manners." A neighbor's teen-aged son willingly helps him exercise Gretchen.

Although there are many practical reasons why people adopt an adult dog instead of buying a puppy, the most common reason is emotional—people enjoy saving a dog's life. Jonathan Baker adopted a Siberian Husky from a South Texas rescue group. "I had

The Pros and Cons of Adopting an Adult Dog

Most dogs available through purebred rescue are adults, although puppies are sometimes available.

The positives about adopting an adult dog are:

1. Adult purebred dogs are what you see; you know how big the dog is, what color it is, the coat length and how much grooming will be required.

2. You can see what the dog's adult personality is (keeping in mind that some things can change when the dog is established in your home).

3. You do not have to go through the time and effort of puppyhood.

4. You will enjoy the feeling of saving the dog's life (adult dogs are generally less likely to be adopted than puppies).

5. Anthropomorphism aside, many rescue dogs have almost a feeling of gratitude for their new home and relationship.

The negatives about adopting an adult dog are:

1. Adopting an adult dog is like buying a used car; you really don't know how it has been treated and that can lead to some surprises.

2. The dog has an unknown health history.

3. There can be some emotional and physical adjustment problems and there are often some training problems.

wanted a dog for quite a while and did a lot of research as to the breeds I was interested in. I finally decided on a Siberian Husky, talked to some breeders and got on the waiting list for a couple of future litters. Then one day I went to a dog show and walked over

An older dog can be the perfect companion for an older person.

to watch the Obedience competition. I saw Janet and her black and silver Siberian work in one of the advanced classes. I was astounded."

He continued his story, "Since I had done a lot of research on this breed, I knew that the kind of Obedience needed for the advanced classes was not really the breed's strong point. So I waited until they were done and then went over to talk. That's when I found out about Siberian Husky Rescue. Janet's dog had been picked up by rescue from a neglectful and possibly abusive owner."

Janet continued with the dog's story, "I had previously adopted a dog from rescue and that relationship was wonderful, so when I was ready for a second dog, of course I called them again. When I heard about this dog, who still had no name, I couldn't bear it. How could a dog grow up without a name? When I saw her, she was feeling better but was still very, very thin. But when I took her home, we bonded quickly and she took to obedience training very well. She really wants to please me. I named her Spunky, because she was and is."

Jonathan said, "After meeting Janet and Spunky, I called the Siberian Rescue group and found that they had several adult dogs ready to be adopted. I made an appointment and fell in love with Racer. He and I have been together for three years now and have a great relationship. I feel good, too, though, knowing that Racer would have died had it not been for me and the rescue group."

CHAPTER 4

Finding Your Rescue Dog

Once you have evaluated your needs and preferences and have narrowed the search to one or two breeds, it's time to start looking for that special dog. There's one out there somewhere just waiting for you to find it.

Finding Rescue Groups

Many rescue organizations have advertisements in the classified section of the newspaper. The Golden Retriever Club of San Diego County has a long-running advertisement in the *San Diego Union-Tribune* that is placed among the ads for Golden puppies. Other groups have ads in dog magazines, such as *Dog Fancy* and *Dog World*. The *AKC Gazette* lists national breed club rescue coordinators in its November issue.

Other rescue groups put flyers out in veterinarians' offices and pet supply stores or even publish their own newsletter. The newspaper *Muttmatchers Messenger* is published by HART, the Humane Animal Rescue Team, in Fillmore, California. The newsletter lists animals available for adoption through HART and other rescue groups and, as an added bonus, maintains listings of rescue organizations in different areas working for several different breeds. Although *Muttmatchers Messenger* is currently only serving the West Coast, other publications of a similar nature are available in other areas. For a copy, check at your local shelter or humane society. Your local shelter or humane society will also probably have a listing of local breed rescue groups.

The American Kennel Club maintains a list of national breed club rescue coordinators. Call them at (212) 696-8246 for the most recent information they have. You can also call the United Kennel Club at (616) 343-9020. Or, if your breed of choice is a rare breed, call the American Rare Breed Association at (202) 722-1232.

Rescue is also on the Internet. Most rescue work is done through networking—people talk to other people about dogs that are available, dogs needing foster homes, people looking for dogs, and so on. The Internet is the ultimate networking tool, and rescuers have taken advantage of it.

Gina Spadafori, the pet columnist for America Online, said, "The Pet Care Forum for America Online has a new area devoted entirely to rescue. Our focus is supporting rescuers and finding new homes for dogs who need them."

Many rescue groups also have home pages on the Internet. For example, the Chow Chow Club of America has a very informative page located at http://www.dvcnet.com/ccci.

To find the breed you are looking for, Spadafori recommends using a search engine such as Yahoo (http://www.yahoo.com) and then entering the name of the breed you're interested in. Many breed clubs have Web pages, and they often list rescue coordinators.

The American Kennel Club also has a Web page (http://www.akc.org). Once you are in the page you can go to your breed and get the breed's rescue contacts.

Project BREED

Project BREED (Breed Rescue Efforts and EDucation) was founded in 1984 by Shirley Weber of Germantown, Maryland, in an effort to increase public awareness of purebred dog rescue groups. Project BREED publishes directories listing breeds, breed descriptions and local, regional and national rescue groups, as well as details about the services those groups offer.

For example, an entry might look like this:

Basset Hound Rescue

Houses homeless Basset Hounds in foster homes.

Dogs spayed or neutered before adoption.

Dogs vaccinated and checked for heartworm before adoption.

Breed information available.

Personal family interview required.

Fenced yard required; dog must live inside as family pet; obedience training recommended.

Post-adoption services.

Dog must be returned to rescue if new owner cannot keep.

The response to the directories has been overwhelming. New rescue groups are sending information, requesting to be listed. Potential adoptees use the directories as a resource for finding that special dog. Plus, shelters and humane societies use the directories as a resource and call rescue groups when a dog of their particular breed is turned in to the shelter.

Project BREED directories may be ordered from Project BREED, PO Box 15888, Chevy Chase, MD 20825-5888 or call (202) 244-0065.

Evaluating the Rescue Group

Rescue groups range from one-person operations to large national groups. No matter what its size, the organization should have some guidelines for accepting dogs into the program and for adopting them out to new homes. Most groups require the dog to be spayed or neutered prior to adoption, or they will have the adopter sign a contract stating that he or she will have the surgery performed soon after adoption.

As with any human endeavor, there are unscrupulous people who try to take advantage of the situation. Some will charge huge fees to take a dog into rescue, others place dogs with known behavior problems into unsuspecting new homes, and so on. Protect yourself by asking to see copies of the contract or other paperwork; ask what fees are normally charged and ask for references.

Make sure you see where the dog you are considering adopting is being kept. Is its area clean and does it appear to be well taken care of? Is the person handling the adoption honest with you about the dog's temperament, how it is with kids, how much training it has had?

Be wary of the group that doesn't ask you any questions, that does not require you to sign an adoption contract or that pushes you to accept a dog quickly. Be wary, too, of the rescue group that is asking a large fee for adopting a dog. You are adopting the dog, not purchasing it, and a large fee may signify that the group (or individual) is trying to make money off the dogs. Most fees (or donations) are used to help cover the costs of spaying or neutering the dogs, vaccinations, grooming, veterinary expenses or other costs incurred while rescuing the dogs. Ask what the fee covers. And be cautious of anyone who asks you to make your check out to them, rather than to the name of the organization they say they represent.

If you have any doubts about the person you are talking to, or about the group as a whole, go somewhere else to find your dog. It's important that you feel comfortable with the rescue volunteer you are working with. This person will be the one to help you find the right dog for you and your family and will be the one to answer your questions. Most rescue groups also provide follow-up counseling to make sure the dog settles into the family well and information on basic dog care and training.

Most rescue volunteers will be more than happy to answer any and all of your questions about their breed and the dogs available for adoption. No question is a stupid one, especially if it is important enough for you to ask it. If you are uncomfortable with this volunteer, the process may not go well. In this type of a situation, don't hesitate to talk to other volunteers or other rescue groups.

However, keep in mind that the people working for most rescue groups are volunteers and usually do this work from their homes. When you call, they may ask to call you back or will ask if they can return your call at another time; if they do, don't get angry. They may be eating dinner, putting the kids to bed or feeding their dogs.

Evaluating the Rescuer

When you contact the rescue group, expect some very pointed questions. You will be asked what you know about the breed, your wants and desires for a dog and your living situation. You will also be asked whether you have owned dogs before and what happened to those dogs. Have you trained a dog before? Do you have kids? Who is going to be responsible for caring for the dog? Do you have elderly family members? A fenced yard? An unfenced pool? The rescuer may want to visit your home to see your fence and yard. You may even be asked about your financial situation.

Don't be offended. Rescuers want to make sure, first of all, that you live where you say you live and that the address isn't a research laboratory, a commercial address or a facility for training junkyard dogs. They want to make sure your yard is safe and secure, with no easy escape route or hidden dangers. If there are questions as to how a particular dog might be with children, they might also want to meet your kids.

Adopting an Older Dog

When most people think of getting a dog, they think only of getting a puppy, usually a young puppy about eight weeks old. However, there are some distinct advantages to adopting an adult, or even an older dog.

Puppies get into a lot of trouble. Most people realize that, but in today's society, where people are working hard and are away from home for long hours at a time, a puppy home alone is not only going to be getting into trouble, but will also be learning bad habits—such as barking—and will be unsocialized. These long hours alone will invariably lead to behavior problems.

There are some advantages to adopting an adult or older dog.

However, many adult dogs are always available for adoption, and these dogs will be past the puppyhood problems. That doesn't mean they won't have problems of their own, though. Many dogs are given up by their first owner because that owner didn't want to deal with problem behavior. Many times problem behavior is not just the dog's fault, it's a combination of factors that include the dog, the owner and the environment—and when a dog goes to a new home, two of those three factors change. The problem may still be present but it will probably be less severe, or different. With loving care, a second chance and some training, that problem behavior may disappear forever.

Many of the adult dogs available for adoption don't have any problems at all; some lost their homes through no fault of their own. Perhaps an owner died or was transferred overseas. Coming from a secure, happy home, these dogs will make wonderful companions.

The inspection and questions are not to satisfy the curiosity of the person asking the questions, but instead are to make sure that your home will be the right one for this breed or particular dog. After all, these dogs have already lost one or more homes—the rescue group's goal now is to find the dog a secure, responsible, *permanent* home. To do that, you will be asked questions—lots of questions. Answer them truthfully. Don't try to say what you think the rescue volunteer wants to hear; instead, answer the questions completely and honestly. It's better for you to end up with the right dog for your family and your situation, and working with the rescue group will help make that happen.

Evaluating the Rescue Dog

Meeting a dog for the first time can be very emotional. Try to control yourself and don't say yes to the very first dog you see. Instead, take a clipboard with a reproduced copy of the evaluation form in this chapter. This evaluation was designed to help rescue volunteers and prospective owners find out as much about each dog as possible. Here's how it works:

Section 1 on Personal History and Section 2 on Personal Identification serve to help identify each dog. If anything is known about the dog's previous home, that can also provide clues to the dog's behavior. The owners may have contributed to the dog's problems by training it incorrectly or not at all. The dog may also have been abused or poorly cared for.

Section 3, Physical Condition, can be answered jointly by you as you examine the dog and by the rescue volunteer who has been caring for the dog. If you have any questions or doubts, ask if a veterinarian can also examine the dog. This section can serve to point out any problems the dog's new owner (you) will have to deal with.

Section 4, Personality/Temperament, is very important because much of the relationship between a dog and its owner is based upon the meshing of two personalities—yours and your dog's. It is also vitally important to identify potential temperament problems, such as placing a very submissive dog in a house full of rowdy teenagers or a dominant, aggressive dog with a shy, less assertive person. Dangerous dogs also need to be identified so that they can be removed from your list of potential pets.

Section 5 on Behavior/Training will help clarify the personality traits identified in the previous section and will demonstrate the dog's knowledge and manners. Section 6 asks what the rescue volunteer caring for the dog thinks of the dog. Hopefully, the volunteer will be honest with you.

Go through all the questions and answer them as best you can. The rescue volunteer who is caring for the dog can also help you answer some of the questions. Don't forget to jot down your reactions, including your feelings about this particular dog. What was your first reaction? How did the dog react to you? Your kids? Did you seem to make a connection with the dog?

After you have completed the evaluation, even if you fell in love with this particular dog don't take the dog home with you. Go home, reread your answers, talk about the dog with your family and with dog-owning friends. Then look at several other dogs. Don't adopt the first dog you see, even if you really liked that dog. To make sure you're choosing the right dog, you need to see more.

Evaluating an Adult Dog

This questionnaire will help you evaluate individual dogs, either for acceptance into a rescue program or for potential adoption. The form helps to pinpoint both potential problem areas in physical health, emotional well-being and behavior. However, it also allows you to note the dog's good points. Completing this the form will help you evaluate each dog as accurately as possible. When you're trying to decide what dog to adopt, you can also compare questionnaires and then, hopefully, choose the dog that is best for you.

1. Personal History
Dog's owner (if known)_____

Address_____

City_____

State_____Zip_____

Phone_____

How did the dog lose its home?_____

Did the dog's first owners cause some of the problems?_____

Where is the dog now?_____

How long has the dog been there?_____

2. Personal Identification
Dog's Name_____

Breed_____

Sex_____ Spayed/Neutered_____

Date_____

Date of Birth_____ Or Approx. Age_____

Color_____ Markings (in detail)_____

_____

_____

_____

Ears (erect, prick, hanging, etc)_____

Tail_____Coat_____

Height at Shoulder_____

Weight_____

Tattoo_____ Microchip_____

3. Physical Condition

Prior to making a commitment to a dog, you will want to know what the dog's health is, what problems it may be facing and what veterinary bills you will have to budget for. Ask for help in making this evaluation from the person fostering the dog or from your veterinarian.

Eyes_____

Nose_____

Ears_____

Mouth/teeth_____

Skin/coat_____

Paws/nails_____

General condition_____

_____

_____

_____

Does the dog have any known or obvious health problems?

_____

_____

_____

Does the dog need immediate care?_____

Does the dog appear to need any major or long-term veterinary care?_____

_____

_____

4. Personality/Temperament

This information is very important when you are trying to match your needs and personality, as well as that of your family, with a dog. If you need a calm, mellow dog who can tolerate babies and toddlers, you don't want to choose an overly dominant, aggressive dog, nor do you want to pick a very fearful, submissive dog.

Where is the dog being observed (home, shelter, veterinarian's office)? (Ideally, the dog should be curious about its surroundings.)_____

_____

_____

In this situation, does the dog appear to be stressed?_____

Does the dog urinate when approached calmly?_____

When approached exuberantly?_____

When approached by a man? A woman? A child?_____

Does the dog snarl? _____

Growl?_____

Show teeth?_____ Try to snap or bite?_____

Does the dog tuck its tail or cower when approached?_____

When petting or playing, does the dog mouth hands?_____

When walking or running, does the dog nip heels or bite pant legs?_____

When greeted, does the dog jump on people?_____

Will the dog allow you to hug it? Does it seem to enjoy the affection?_____

Check those that seem to be most appropriate:
Is the dog:

_____Aggressive/threatening

_____Protective but not threatening

_____Wildly active

_____Very active

_____Self confident

_____Steady/stable

_____Calm

_____Concerned

_____Cautious/reserved

_____Withdrawn/shy

_____Fearful/afraid

_____Nonsocial/feral

5. Behavior/Training

Is the dog house-broken?_____

Whistle or click your tongue; does the dog look up at you? (A stable, friendly dog should look up easily. A frightened dog will look away or look at you sideways. An aggressive dog will try and stare you down.)_____

Walk away from the dog and encourage it to follow you. (Ideally, it should follow you. A dominant dog will dash ahead or try to block your path. A submissive dog will cower. An unsocialized dog will ignore you.) _____

Does the dog appear to have had any training?_____

Does the dog recognize and respond (in some manner) to: Heel, sit, down, stay or come?_____

How does the dog behave when walking on a leash?_____

_____

_____

_____

What bad habits does the dog have? (chewing, digging, barking, etc.)_____

_____

_____

Does the dog play with a ball? A Frisbee? _____

What does the dog's caretaker or foster owner think of it?

_____

_____

_____

6. Your General Comments:

_____

_____

_____

_____

Meeting a dog for the first time can be very emotional. Give yourself a few days to really think it over before you choose your special dog.

After evaluating several dogs, go through your notes and see which dog seems to be the best dog for you, both logically and emotionally. Ask the people working with the rescue group for their opinion, if they haven't already offered it. Which dog do they think will be best for you?

Choosing exactly the right dog for you can be hard. An impulse decision is rarely the right one; neither is a totally emotional one. Yet a decision based totally upon cold, hard facts isn't right either—too much of the relationship with a dog is emotional. Instead, make a decision based on sound research and facts, with the added boost of your emotional reaction to the dog. That balance is usually right.

When You've Found Your Dog

When you have found the right dog for you, the rescue group will ask you to sign an adoption contract. They do so for many reasons, but the most important is to make sure you and other potential dog owners understand that this dog is important, both to the rescue group and to you.

Below is a sample adoption contract. The Yankee Siberian Husky Rescue Service uses this agreement whenever a Siberian Husky is adopted from their program. The first part of the agreement identifies the dog being adopted and the adoption fee (many rescue groups ask for a donation to cover the costs of spaying, neutering, vaccinations or other expenses incurred while in the group's care).

The second section is a liability release and is fairly standard among most rescue groups. The sections that follow list the terms of the adoption, including a guarantee of return: If the dog cannot be kept by the adoptive owner for any reason, it must be returned to the rescue group. Again, this is a standard term in almost all adoption contracts (if it isn't, take a closer look at the group offering the dog).

Other terms include requirements that the dog be vaccinated regularly, licensed, tested for heartworm and given preventives, groomed regularly and receive all the care necessary for good health and happiness.

The Yankee Siberian Husky Rescue Service also reserves the right to follow up on this adoption by checking back to make sure the dog is being cared for properly; if the dog is not, the group reserves the right to take back the dog. This, too, is standard for all rescue groups.

Other rescue groups have additional terms in their contracts. The Abandoned Terrier Rescue Association has a paragraph that reads, "Terriers are known to have the potential for aggression with other dogs. Knowing this, I agree to all necessary and appropriate steps to keep this terrier confined in an adequately fenced yard and to always keep the terrier on leash when out of the yard."

The Aussie Rescue & Placement Helpline also requires that the adopted Australian Shepherd will not be kept as an outside yard dog, explaining that these dogs must be inside with their

Yankee Siberian Husky Rescue Service Adoption Agreement and Release

Date _____

The Yankee Siberian Husky Rescue Service (YSHRS), in consideration of the sum of $_____, releases the full responsibility and ownership for Dog's Name_____
Description _____
to the undersigned adopter.

The undersigned adopter does hereby release and covenant to hold harmless The Yankee Siberian Husky Rescue Service (YSHRS) and its members and officers from any claims, damages, costs or actions incurred as a result of this adoption or caused by the actions of the dog transferred herein.

The adopter further agrees to abide by the terms of adoption, listed below:

1. Transfer of ownership: This dog will not be transferred to any other person by the adopter. If, for any reason, the adoption is not satisfactory, the dog will be returned to the Yankee Siberian Husky Rescue Service.

2. Health: The dog will receive annual vaccinations as prescribed by a veterinarian in order to assure and maintain good health. The dog will be licensed in accordance with state and local ordinances. The dog will be tested annually for heartworm and given heartworm preventives as prescribed by the veterinarian.

3. Care: The adopter accepts full responsibility for maintaining a reasonable level of care for this dog, including food, water, grooming, adequate sanitation, exercise, attention, safety and shelter.

4. Control: The dog will not be allowed to run loose off the adopter's property, and will be on leash when not within the boundaries of the adopter's property.

5. Reservation of rights: The Yankee Siberian Husky Rescue Service reserves the right to an ongoing review of this adoption and to follow up on any complaints or reports, to protect the welfare of this dog. If the terms of this agreement are not satisfactorily upheld by the adopter, and/or if any misrepresentations have been made to YSHRS in order to obtain the dog, the YSHRS reserves the right to void this agreement and demand the return of the dog to the YSHRS by the adopter.

Signed this _____ day of _____ 19____.

Adopter's signature _____

Printed Name _____

Address_____

City_____State_____Zip_____

Home Phone _____Work Phone _____

Countersigned YSHRS Volunteer _____

Printed Name _____

YSHRS Position _____

Reprinted with permission of the Yankee Siberian Husky Rescue Service, Northfield, Massachusetts.

family. Another adoption agreement states that the adopted dog will not be used in medical or animal experimentation, nor will the dog be subjected to cruelty, abuse or neglect.

When you have read and signed the contract, the rescue volunteer will countersign it and you will both receive a copy. The volunteer will also give you information about what the dog has been eating, its vaccination records, the date of its spay or neuter, and any other information you will need to know before bringing your new dog home. Make sure you ask every question you can think of and understand all the answers. Take notes if you need to; you may be so excited about your new dog that you forget something.

• •

CHAPTER 5

Before You Bring Your Rescue Dog Home

You've got some things to do before you bring home your new dog. Not only do you need to dog-proof your house and yard, but you'll also need to do some shopping for dog food and for supplies. Finally, you will need to find a few professionals to work with you and your dog during your future together. Doing all these things before you bring home your new dog will allow you to spend time with your dog, getting to know it instead of running errands and panicking at last-minute crises.

Dog-Proofing Your World

In order to prevent problems, you need to look at your home, yard and garage very carefully to make sure there is nothing there to tempt your dog. When you are dog-proofing your world, never assume that the dog will not notice, taste, chew on or knock over something. No one can second-guess what might attract a dog on any given day. A stressed, lonely or bored dog might chew on the corner of the chaise lounge cushion, pull out some stuffing and then find that it's fun, so he pulls out some more. Before you know it, he's destroyed all of the cushions and has had a great time doing it! Prevention is the name of the game, especially until you get to know the dog and can start some training.

Walk through your house and put away anything that is breakable, chewable or attractive to dogs. Do you have some knick-knacks or collectibles that you treasure? If so, lift them out of reach or pack them away. You need to assume that your new dog will not know any household rules when he joins your family. He may like to chew on things and may not understand that those collectibles she just destroyed were given to you by your great-grandmother and that you consider them irreplaceable, so put them away.

Crawl around your house on your hands and knees, trying to look at things from the dog's eye level. What looks interesting? Put it away. Make sure telephone and electrical cords are tucked away, too, so that they cannot be pulled or chewed.

Close all the closet doors so that your good shoes don't get chewed.

Pick up anything that is tail-height, too, if you are adopting a breed with a tail. It's amazing how much power a happy tail has. A German Shepherd can clear a coffee table with one quick swipe!

Baby gates that can be set up across hallways are a good investment. By limiting your new dog's freedom so that he stays in the same room you are in, you can make sure he doesn't sneak off to have a house-training accident or to chew on something he shouldn't.

Eventually you will be able to bring your knickknacks and collectibles back out, but not until you are sure that your new dog understands what is hers to play with or chew on and what is yours. Chapter 6 will go into more detail about preventing problems and dog training.

You will need to dog-proof your yard just as you do your house, especially if your dog is going to spend any time alone in the yard; a dog left alone can be very curious, will get bored and can be very destructive.

Start by examining your fence. Make sure it is secure, that there are no loose boards and no holes under the fence. Even a small hole can tempt a dog, who will then enlarge the hole and possibly escape from the yard. Make sure there is nothing up against the fence that a dog could climb up onto and then climb or jump over the fence.

If you have a pool, make sure it is fenced off so that the dog cannot fall in. Many, many dogs drown in pools each year because it can be extremely difficult for them to climb out when their coat is waterlogged. Even dogs who swim with their owners and appear to know where the steps are often panic when they are alone in the pool. So don't take any chances—protect the dog from the pool just as you would a young child.

When dog-proofing the yard, make sure you pick up and put away all your yard and garden tools, insecticides, fertilizers, snail bait, gopher poison and any other substance that could hurt the dog. Put away the grill, the charcoal and the lighter fluid. Again, a bored, curious or lonely dog can get into a lot of trouble, so prevention is the key.

If your yard is nicely landscaped and you're concerned that the dog might harm it, you might want to build a dog run. A dog run can be the dog's own place and is not cruel to the dog as long as she gets plenty of time out of the run when you're at home.

Enclosing the long, narrow part of the yard that runs along the side of your house could make a good dog run. Again, make sure the fence is secure and clean up all the garden supplies, tools and trash that might be stored there. Make sure the dog will have shade and water in some part of the run all day.

If you're not going to build a run but want to protect your vegetable or flower gardens, put a fence around them. Your new dog isn't going to understand why he's not allowed to sample your ripening tomatoes or strawberries, so make them inaccessible. If you have some potted plants, pick them up out of reach for a while.

Many dog owners would like to let their dog have access to the garage from the backyard so that the dog can have some shelter while they're at work. Unfortunately, the garage can be a very dangerous place for dogs. All of the garden fertilizers and insecticides, as well as all of the chemicals for car maintenance and repair, are deadly to dogs.

If you would like to let your dog in the garage, fence off a small section of the garage where the dog can have shelter but will be away from the dangers in the rest of the garage. Make this section accessible from the door leading to the dog's area in the backyard, and then dog-proof it thoroughly, removing anything even remotely dangerous.

Time to Go Shopping!

Your new dog will need some supplies. First, of course, is food. Find out what the rescue group has been feeding him and buy a supply of the same kind. Many dogs cannot change foods without getting an upset stomach or diarrhea, so have a supply on hand of the food your new dog is used to eating.

However, if you prefer a different brand, buy both and take about three weeks to switch her over to the new food. Feed 75

Do You Know What Can Poison Your Dog?

Some common household products can be extremely dangerous to your dog. When dog-proofing your house and garage, check for these substances and make sure they are out of reach or locked away. As an added note, most of these products are also dangerous to children.

Car products
Antifreeze
Brake fluid
Gasoline
Windshield washer
  detergent

**Cleaners and
  chemicals**
Bleach
Boric acid
Disinfectants
Drain cleaner
Paint and paint remover

Soaps and detergents
Varnish

Gardening products
Fertilizers
Fungicides
Furniture polish
Herbicides
Insecticides

In the medicine chest
Acetaminophen
Aspirin
Deodorants

Make sure all poisonous products are put away and that cupboard doors latch securely.

Elsewhere in the house

- Chocolate
- Insecticides
- Matches
- Mothballs
- Rat, mouse or gopher poison

Indoor and outdoor plants

- Almond
- Amaryllis
- Apricot
- Asparagus Fern
- Avocado Leaves
- Azalea
- Bittersweet
- Bitterweed
- Black Locust
- Bluebonnets
- Bracken Fern
- Castor Bean
- China Berry
- Chokecherry
- Cockle Burr
- Creeping Fig
- Daffodil
- Delphinium
- Diffenbachia
- Ficus Benjamina
- Foxglove
- Goldenrod
- Hemlock
- Holly
- Japanese Plum
- Jasmine
- Jerusalem Cherry
- Jimson Weed
- Kafir
- Larkspur
- Locoweed
- Lily of the Valley
- Milkweed
- Mock Orange
- Morning Glory
- Nightshade
- Oleander
- Peyote
- Poinsettia
- Pothos
- Privet
- Rhubarb
- Soapberry
- Sorghum
- Toadstool
- Tomato Vine
- Wild Cherry
- Yew Tree

percent old food, 25 percent new food the first week; half and half the second week and 25 percent old food, 75 percent new food the third week. By making the change gradually, you can prevent your dog from developing gastrointestinal upset.

Obviously, your dog will need a bowl to eat out of and a water bowl or two. At least one water bowl should be the unspillable kind so that if you are away from home for a number of hours, your dog won't get thirsty. Many dog owners prefer stainless steel bowls because they're sturdy, difficult for the dog to chew and are dishwasher safe. However, what you use is strictly up to you.

Your dog will also need a leash and a collar. The leash should be strong enough to hold your dog safely when you go for a walk and should be comfortable for your hands. The collar should be a fabric or leather buckle collar that your dog will wear at all times. This collar can have his identification tag and license (when you

get it) attached to it. Most pet supply stores have order blanks for identification tags; if you know your new dog's name, you can order this before you bring your dog home.

The next thing your new dog will need is a kennel crate. This will serve as your dog's bed at night, or when you may need to leave him in the house alone. It will be her place of refuge when she's tired or sick, and a place of security when you travel (for more on crate training, see Chapter 6). There are different

Your garage can be a dangerous place for your dog.

kinds of kennel crates, wire or plastic, but whichever type you choose, it should be big enough for your dog to stand up, turn around and lie down.

Your new dog will also need some grooming tools—which ones depends upon the breed of dog. For some coat lengths and types, you may need a stiff wire comb, a slicker brush, a soft bristled brush or a long bladed mat splitter. Each of these tools has a different purpose, so to make sure you have what you will need to care for your dog properly, ask the breed rescue volunteer who is caring for your new dog what you should have on hand.

Your new dog will also need some toys. You can pick out a few things for him to chew on before bringing him home, but then take him with you to the pet supply store and let him choose a few things himself. On his leash, of course, let him walk around in the store and sniff some of the chewies and toys that are available. Watch him while you do this and see the joy in his eyes.

Finding the Right Professionals

There are three professionals you will need to help you as your new dog joins your family. A veterinarian will be in charge of your dog's health care, a groomer will be able to help you keep your dog's skin and coat healthy and a dog trainer can help you train your dog and establish some household rules. Each of these professionals has a wealth of knowledge that can help with your dog. Establishing a working relationship with each of them before your dog comes home will make the entire transition much easier, especially if your dog needs some care right away.

Finding the right professional to work with can take some time, which is why it's a good idea to start looking at the same time you begin your search for a dog. Ask friends, family, neighbors and co-workers who they recommend. Jot down the names they mention and the reasons why. Do one or two names come up more often than others? When you have several names for each of the professions, call up and make appointment to talk to these people. An appointment is necessary because these are busy professionals, and if you want some of their time be prepared to pay for it, at least the charge for an office visit.

At your appointment, tell the professional that you will soon be adopting a dog, what type of dog he is and anything you know about him. Tell the pro what help you anticipate needing and ask what they offer as professional services. What are their office hours? What are their facilities like? Can you see the facilities? What are their charges? What do they do in case of emergencies? And last but certainly not least, what do they think of the breed you are considering? Make notes during and after the interview before you forget, so that you know who said what, where and when.

After interviewing several different professionals, look over your notes. Which veterinarian, groomer and trainer did you feel most comfortable with? Whose staff was professional yet friendly? Who is normally available, at least by answering machine or service, in case of an emergency?

When you finally choose a professional, go back to their office and fill out the needed paperwork to set up a client file. Then, when you have brought your dog home, you can arrange a get acquainted visit.

Time to Spare

Your new dog will need to spend some time with you, especially when you first bring her home. You might want to arrange some vacation time so that you don't have to run off to work the day after you bring your dog home. Or plan to pick the dog up the evening before a three-day weekend.

Your new dog will also need time with you after your vacation is over and after the long weekend, so look at your schedule with a critical eye and plan ahead for when you can spend time with your dog. Keep in mind that a dog is a social animal who needs

Bronte (left) and Dixie now enjoy the good life. (Courtesy of Ben Miller)

A Tale of Two Beauties

Bronte and Dixie, two beautiful red Siberian Huskies with blue eyes, both found new homes through the Yankee Siberian Husky Rescue in Northfield, Massachusetts. Both dogs settled into their new home easily with few adjustment problems. Their new owner, Ben Miller, felt that both had been obedience trained previously,

companionship every single day. Dogs who spend hours alone in the backyard invariably develop behavior problems caused by boredom, loneliness and lack of simulation and exercise. Honestly evaluate your current time commitments. If you will have an ongoing problem scheduling time, you may want to rethink your decision to get a dog.

but he did some refresher training anyway. "Both dogs are better than we could have hoped for. The Rescue group was and continues to be very helpful with any problems," Miller said.

As the name implies, Yankee Siberian Husky Rescue works with only one breed. The group earns money through donations, adoption fees and a small store that is set up at club functions. People giving up Siberians or people wishing to adopt one can find out about the group through their flyers which are displayed at local veterinarians' offices and the local shelters. The shelters have the organization's telephone number, too, as do the rescue listings in the area.

The group screens dogs before it takes them into the adoption program and screens people before allowing them to adopt a dog. It maintains a foster home network and also follows up after an adoption, providing adjustment support to the new owner. If the adoption doesn't work out, Yankee Siberian Husky Rescue will take the dog back.

Miller says, "Adopting an adult dog eliminates all of the puppy problems, plus you have a better idea of what you're getting. Most importantly, I like the idea of giving a dog a second chance at life."

To find a local Siberian Husky Rescue program, call the Siberian Husky Club of America rescue coordinator at (908) 782-2089.

CHAPTER 6

••

What to Expect and How to Handle It

Your new dog's rescuer or foster owners have probably told you quite a bit about your dog. However, if you still have questions, make sure you ask them. Does your new dog walk on a leash? What food does he eat? Is she trained to use a kennel crate? Does he like to be brushed or does he fight it? Does she try to climb fences if she's left outside alone? What words does he understand? Dinner? Hungry? Food? Cookie? Biscuit? Walk? Outside? Go potty? Ball? Toy? The more you know about your new dog, the easier the transition can be, so make sure you ask plenty of questions.

The First Few Days

How your new dog reacts to joining your household will depend upon many factors, including the dog's personality and temperament, his previous experiences and your home environment. If the dog is by nature happy-go-lucky, was well loved and socialized as a puppy and attended training classes, then he will probably join your household with little emotional stress. If she was strongly bonded to her first owner, she may grieve a while but should settle in well. If the dog has been neglected or mistreated, is more serious, fearful or shy, or is a worrier, then there may be some adjustment problems.

If your new dog spent his first months or years in a backyard and was never socialized to the world outside the yard, leaving that yard, going to a foster home and then to your home could be very emotionally trying. Just the change in location can cause stress. Dogs are by nature very territorial. When you adopt your new dog and bring him home, the new territory alone will cause stress, especially if you have other pets at home that already claim your home as their own territory. The people who make up your family or household are all strangers, too. Your household routine is unknown and the smells, noises and sights are all different.

For the first few days, don't make too many demands on your new dog. This is not the time to have company over, to start obedience classes or to go for marathon walks. Instead, let her get used to her new home. Let her walk around, under your supervision, of course, and let her discover where she is. She may investigate all the rooms of the house and explore the backyard. As she explores, if she sticks her nose into something you would rather she leave alone, tell her so, "Ack! Leave it!" and encourage her to walk away.

To teach her where you want her to relieve herself, go outside with her and walk her to that area. Just stand there (this is not the time for play) and when she relieves herself, tell her, "Good girl to go potty!" (or use whatever vocabulary you wish her to learn).

Don't force your new dog to involve himself in the household activities. He may be grieving, worried, wary, fearful or shy. After all, your household is strange to him. Just let him watch and when he does start to involve himself, don't make a big deal out of it or you may scare him back into hiding.

If you have another dog and the two seem to get along, let your new dog follow the resident dog around. Dogs can learn a lot by watching each other, and your new dog will see where the resident dog relieves herself, where the toys are and where the coolest place to relax is on a summer afternoon. The new dog will also feel the resident dog's calmness, happiness and security and that can go a long way towards making the new dog feel at home. (For more on multi-pet households, see Chapter 7.)

Keep in mind that every dog is different. Because of that, the adjustment period for each dog is different, too. Some dogs may settle into their new home within days, happy and secure. Other dogs may take weeks before they feel comfortable. Take your time with your new dog, be patient and be kind.

Making the Transition Easier

The first week or so following your dog's adoption is an important time. He is in a new environment filled with unfamiliar smells, new people and perhaps, other animals. He will be confused, stressed, possibly submissive and frightened, maybe even a little over-stimulated. This is a great time to cement your relationship, to help him bond with you and to start regarding you as his leader. This is also a good time to teach your dog the rules of your house—rules that might be totally different from those in his first home.

Just as you don't want to force your new dog to become involved in your household activities, don't force her to love you, either. Let her come to you, both physically and emotionally, when she's ready. If you try to force her, you may just drive her away.

There are, however, a few things you can do to speed up the bonding process. First of all, let your new dog spend time with you as you go through your normal daily routine. Instead of putting him out in the backyard, keep him in the house with you as you wash dishes, do the laundry, or work at the computer. Encourage him to follow you from room to room but other than that, don't do much else. Let him watch and listen.

Second, set up a regular routine for things that have to do with her. Dogs are creatures of habit, and when your new dog joined your household she was left without the security of her normal routine, whatever it might have been. So set up a new routine for her. Let her know that each day at a specific time she will eat, go outside to go potty, play ball, go for another walk and so on.

Third, make time every day for exercise. If your new dog has a high energy level, exercise twice a day might be even better. Exercise is a great way to stimulate the body to release endorphins, which naturally battle stress and depression. You can do a variety of things for exercise, but one of the easiest and best for a new dog is to play retrieving games. Throw the tennis ball or Frisbee for him until he's panting and tired. Retrieving games are also fun for you: You will laugh when you throw the Frisbee badly; you'll praise your new dog when he makes a good catch; and you'll cheer when he returns the ball to you. It's fun and there's no stress involved at all. As a side benefit, when he's had a chance to use up all that stored energy, your new dog will also be less apt to get into trouble.

Set up a place for your new dog in your bedroom so she can sleep close to you; not in your bed, but close to your bed. What works for many people is to take the night stand out of the bedroom and put the crate in its place, right next to your bed. Put your clock, your book and so forth on top of the crate. This way your new dog can smell you and hear you for eight hours. As you sleep, she is close to you, getting to know you, bonding with you.

Crate Training Can Work

When a pet professional recommends that a dog owner use a kennel crate to train a dog, the owner's first reaction is usually, "What? Put my dog in a cage? In a jail? No way!" However, a crate is not a jail and in many circumstances it can be a very effective training tool.

Many dogs like to sleep in close, confined places—under the foot of the recliner, under the end table or under the back porch. Dogs are den animals by nature and they often feel protected in small places; no one is going to sneak up on them or step on them. A kennel crate allows you to use this desire for security to train your dog.

With the right approach, a crate can become a haven for your dog.

Once the dog is comfortable with the kennel crate, it becomes the dog's bed, her place of refuge when she's tired, overwhelmed or sick. The kennel crate is wonderful when the dog needs to travel or when you must move; the dog is usually not as worried about traveling when she's in her place of security.

The kennel crate can also prevent problems from occurring. If your new dog likes to chew on furniture or raid the trash can, using the kennel crate to confine the dog can prevent those things from happening until you can teach the dog what is allowed and what is not.

Last, but certainly not least, spend some quiet time with your dog. If you have adopted a quiet, shy or fearful dog, or a even a more outgoing dog who seems somewhat shell-shocked by the changes in his life, this quiet time can be wonderful for reassuring the dog that all is well. With the dog in the same room with you, turn on the television low or get out a book you've been wanting to read. Sit or lay on the floor and read or watch television. Don't call the dog to you; in fact, most of the time you're better off just ignoring him. When he starts moving your way, don't make eye contact with him, although you can softly acknowledge him, "Hi, sweetie." When he moves close to you or settles himself next to you, scratch behind his ear or rub his tummy but don't make a big deal out of it. Keep it calm and quiet.

Establishing Your Leadership

As your dog starts to adapt to your household routine and is getting more comfortable with her new life, it's time to start establishing your role as your dog's new leader. Dogs, as social pack animals, need a leader they respect to whom they can look to for guidance and security. As your dog's new owner, that becomes your job.

Some very simple things can help establish you in this role. First of all, carry yourself like a leader. Stand tall, with your head up. When you pet your dog, lean over her to pet her and hug her to you. In your dog's language, the dominant dog demonstrates that dominance by putting a paw or chin on the shoulder of the less dominant dog. By leaning over your dog as you pet him, you are essentially doing the same thing. Don't sit on the floor and pet him from underneath; in your dog's language that is submissive.

Don't pet your new dog too much. Talk to her, that's fine, and pet her when she has done something right, but don't fawn over her. If your new dog is at all dominant in personality, she may think petting is her due and if you pet too much, she will think you are submissive to her.

You always eat first. Again, in pack terminology the leader also eats first and gets the choicest foods. So you eat breakfast or dinner first, then your new dog eats. If you need to feed him and it's not time for your meal yet, sit down and have an apple or a few carrots, then feed your dog. And of course, while you're eating your new dog is not to beg; he should wait quietly.

You should also go through doorways first and then give permission for your dog to follow you. This is important both to establish dominance and to make sure your new dog doesn't dash out the door and run away or get hit by a car. If you have stairs in your house, the same applies here, too. You should always go up the stairs first and have your new dog follow you up the stairs. It establishes your authority, and it's a lot safer than having a dog bound past you on the stairs.

As your new dog gets to know the house and the routine, let your dog know what is right and what is wrong. If he starts to jump up on the sofa, tell him, "Ack! No! Get down." If he doesn't understand that vocabulary yet, go over to him and gently pull him off the sofa as you repeat the command. Encourage him to curl up on his bed or blanket. Later, when you see him voluntarily go to his blanket, quietly praise him, "Good boy to go to bed!"

Teach your dog that he must sit for everything he wants. Have him sit when you hand him a treat. Have him sit when you reach down to pet him. Have him sit when he brings you the ball to throw. When you have him sit for everything, you are showing him that you are setting the rules for his behavior and that he needs to work for you. Having him sit is a very easy job, yet it conveys a much bigger message.

Now is also the time to establish some household rules. The easiest way to do this is to have a family meeting and make a list. What is important? Does Mom want the new dog to stay out of the kitchen when she's cooking? Maybe it would be better to teach the new dog to stay out of the kitchen all the time. Is the dog to be allowed on the furniture? Or perhaps just on the old couch in the family room?

Make a list of the household rules, both do's and don'ts. Then go through that list again and work up a vocabulary so that as the dog is taught these new rules, everyone is using the same words. If the dog jumps on the sofa and Mom says, "Get off the couch!"

while Dad says, "Down!" and Junior says, "Rover, get down before Mom catches you!" then the dog will be totally confused and will never really learn what the right command is and what is expected of him.

Household Rules

Here are some sample household rules that you may want to consider for your new dog, along with some vocabulary suggestions. You can use these as a guideline, but remember that the words you use are not important; being consistent is. Post your rules and vocabulary in a prominent place so everyone in the household will be consistent.

Household Rules and Commands

The dog is NOT allowed to:

Jump on people: "No jump"
Get off the furniture: "Off"
Wander through the kitchen: "Out of the kitchen"
Sniff the trash cans: "Leave it"
Sniff the cat litter box: "Leave it"
Dash out any open door or gate: "Wait"
Chase the cat or other pets: "No chase" or "Leave it"

The dog should:

Sit for everything (treats, toys, petting): "Sit. Good dog!"
Lie down and be still; stop pestering: "Lie down. Stay"
Go outside: "Go outside"
Find a spot to relieve himself: "Go potty" or "Find a place"
Go to your kennel crate: "Go to bed"
Find your ball (or other toy): "Find your ball"
Jump in the car: "In the car"

Hopefully, everyone in your household wanted a dog when you decided to adopt your new dog, because that household unity is very important right now. Just as with the dog's new vocabulary, if even one person in your family decides to ignore the new dog's household rules or obedience training, the dog will be confused. Consistency is very important.

Some Common Problems

There are some behaviors that are very common in newly adopted dogs, so don't be disturbed if your new dog does some of these things. However, just because they are common and your dog does them does not mean you should accept them. Teach your dog what to do and what not to do.

Jumping on people: Your new dog may jump up on you to try and greet you face to face. This is a natural greeting behavior for dogs and your new dog might do it to try and lick your face, a submissive gesture. Don't correct her harshly. Instead, simply have her sit and pet her while she's sitting.

Jumping on furniture: He may try to jump on the living room furniture, the kitchen counters or the dining room table. Let your new dog drag his leash in the house while you supervise him and when he misbehaves, use the leash to stop him as you tell him, "No! Off the furniture!" Pet him when he has all four feet on the floor.

Stealing food: If your dog has ever gone hungry, she may try to steal food. Many dogs have a hard time distinguishing between things that are hers and things that are yours. Keep all food out of reach, trash cans emptied and dirty dishes put away for a while, and teach her what she is allowed to touch and what is off limits.

Establish house rules about the furniture and then be consistent.

House-training accidents: A dog may be very well house-trained in one house, but your house is different; it's not the same house, the people and the daily routine are different. These things can all affect house-training. Take him outside, show him where to go and praise him when he does. Supervise him in the house and don't let him sneak off to have an accident.

House-Training an Adult Dog

Adding an adult dog to the household is much like buying a used car: You will often inherit someone else's problems.

Many dogs are given up by their owners because the dog has never been properly or thoroughly house-trained. The good news is that this problem can usually be solved.

The first thing you need to do is set up a regular routine. Make sure the dog goes outside first thing in the morning and last thing at night, and about every three hours in between. Your new dog will also need to relieve himself after eating, after exercise and after waking up. Although adult dogs can hold their bowels and bladder much longer than puppies can, this schedule is necessary to show the dog what to do and where, and to prevent any accidents in the house.

Go outside with your new dog when you send him out to relieve himself. Don't play with him or even talk to him. Just take him to the place where you want him to go and stand there quietly. When he does relieve himself, wait until he's almost done (so you don't interrupt him) and tell him, very quietly, "Good boy to go potty!" (or use whatever vocabulary you wish, but be sure to say something very positive).

Make sure your new dog is on a regular feeding schedule, too. If he eats at a specific time each day, it will be easier to get his bowels on a regular schedule.

Don't let your new dog have free run of the house during house-training. If you do, it's too easy for him to sneak off to another room to have an accident instead of going outside. Keep in mind he wants to be with you, close to you, and he may not want to take the time to go outside. Also, he may not know how to ask to go out. So keep him in the room with you and close other doors or put up baby gates to keep him close.

At night, have your dog sleep in his crate right next to your bed. When he's confined in a crate, he can't wander off to have an accident or two in other rooms. The crate is his bed, and because he won't want to soil the bed that he has to spend the night in, he will develop bowel and bladder control or figure out how to tell you he needs to go out. Plus, by being close to you, he gets a chance to bond with you.

If you find an accident, don't rub his nose in it. The act of relieving himself is not what was wrong, it was where he relieved himself that was wrong. If you rub his nose in it, he may associate that punishment with relieving himself and then will get sneaky. He'll go only when you're not around, and not only will he have more accidents, but he won't ask to go out and you will never have a chance to praise him for going in the right place.

If you catch him in the act, say, "Ack! No," and take him outside to finish. When he does, be sure to praise him. If you don't catch him at it, just clean up the mess and keep trying.

If you feel that your new dog is now house-trained, don't slack up. Keep doing what you're doing. After all, it's working, right? As the dog proves himself, very gradually give him more freedom, a room at a time. If he does well and continues to ask to go outside and has no accidents, great. If he backslides, go back to the stricter routine. Most dogs, even well house-trained dogs, backslide once in a while right after moving to a new home.

If the dog has been house-trained and suddenly backslides, there is usually a reason. Is the dog on any medication? Does the dog have a bladder infection? Sometimes geriatric dogs don't have full control of their bladder anymore. Make sure you consult your veterinarian about any sudden changes in a normally well house-trained dog; it may be health related.

Separation anxiety: Once your dog has started to bond with you, you may find that she's following you everywhere, even to the bathroom! Many rescued dogs go through a period of anxiousness where they want to be with you constantly. Although this may be flattering at first, it's unrealistic.

Be patient with your dog. When you do have to leave her, keep it quiet and low-key. Just before you leave, give her a treat or a special toy and then go, without making a big fuss. When you come home, keep that low-key, too.

Most dogs outgrow their separation anxiety. However, if it seems to be getting worse instead of better, call your rescue volunteer or a local dog behaviorist in your area for some personal help.

Koda the Escape Artist

Tim Raines and Ginny McLaurin of Atlanta, Georgia, adopted Koda, an Alaskan Malamute, after losing one of their Siberian Huskies to cancer. Koda, a four-year-old, 130-pound dog, had been left in a backyard with little human contact. When he was adopted by Tim and Ginny, he was desperate for attention.

This caused some problems initially, as Koda learned how to escape from his new yard. One day in particular, he escaped four times. Afraid that he would scare the neighborhood children, be stolen or be hit by a car, Tim and Ginny consulted with the rescue group volunteers. They suggested setting up a kennel in the basement, where Koda could stay safely while Tim and Ginny were at work. Problem solved.

Koda, a sweet dog by nature, became the star of his obedience training class. With exposure and socialization, he became better around strange dogs and people. Ginny says Koda is such a handsome dog that out in public, he has been known to stop traffic. Meanwhile, Tim and Ginny say they love him very much, even with his personality quirks. Soon Koda's lonely years will be only a distant memory.

Koda (in front) and his friend Dusty relax during TV time in the evening. (Courtesy of Tim Raines)

Wild behavior in the house: Your new dog may start running and playing as a means of using up excess energy or of expressing stress. However, your house is not a gymnasium; limit the rough play to outside (be sure your kids follow this rule!), and be sure you're giving your dog plenty of appropriate exercise.

Give Your Dog Some Time

As your new dog joins your household and family, she may have a lot to learn. Set some rules, teach her what life in this household is like, but also be patient. Give her time to adjust.

• •

CHAPTER 7

Introducing Your Dog to Your Other Pets

Throughout this chapter you'll see the same message over and over: Just be careful. Although dogs have been domesticated for 20,000 years, they are still, by nature, predators and as such can be fast, sneaky and deadly. But that doesn't mean you can't have any other pets when you have a dog. That's not true at all. Dogs and other pets can coexist quite peacefully when the dog has learned to respect the other pets. Don't let your dog chase the other animals, and make sure the other pets are adequately protected from your dog. Although special relationships can develop between animals of totally different species, it's safest to allow those relationships to develop slowly under supervised conditions, rather than to tempt disaster.

Your Dog at Home

Introducing a new dog to your resident dog must be done with tact and understanding so that the relationship can get off to a good start. If the two dogs get along, a new dog can greatly increase the quality of the resident dog's life. The new dog can be a friend; someone to romp, wrestle and play hide-the-bone with. If the resident dog is already well trained it can serve as a good example to your new dog, showing the newcomer the rules of the house and yard.

However, adding a second dog to the household is not always easy. Your resident dog already has a relationship with you and considers your home and yard to be its territory. Although some dogs will readily accept another dog, some will view the newcomer as a threat to their territory and a rival for your affections. Depending upon the personality of each dog, it may take some time to establish peaceful coexistence.

For these reasons, it's important that you first introduce the dogs in neutral territory. Find a park or schoolyard that is fairly quiet where neither dog has been before so you can allow the dogs to meet each other and neither will have to defend its territory.

Have a friend or family member meet you at this location with your resident dog while you go pick up your new dog. With both dogs on leash, let them sniff each other while you talk to your friend. Keep an eye on the dogs, but don't intervene unless there's trouble. Be casual about this; if you're worried and stressed both dogs will sense it and will assume something is wrong with the other dog, and you'll end up with a dog fight. Control your emotions.

During the introduction, especially for the first few minutes, don't hold the leashes tight on the dogs' necks. Many dogs are much braver (or make a show of being braver) when they feel a tight, restraining leash. Instead, let each leash hang loose as the dogs get to know each other.

Also, don't make a big fuss over either dog. If you show too much affection to your new dog during the introduction, your resident dog will be jealous. If you show too much affection to the resident dog, the new dog may feel overwhelmed and left out. Concentrate on watching the dogs and talking to your friend.

As the dogs get to know each other, there may be some posturing. The resident, or dominant dog may stand on tiptoes and put its chin on the other dog's shoulder. The submissive dog may lick the older dog's muzzle or may roll over and bare its belly. Or one dog may play bow, inviting the other to play by lowering its front end and wagging its tail. If both dogs are mature adults, there may

Dogs sort out their pack order through body language. The submissive dog may roll over and show her belly, while the dominant dog may stand over her.

be a little more testing to see which dog is the more dominant. There may even be some growling. That's okay, it's all normal.

Don't interfere unless it looks like the posturing is turning into a fight. If the posturing and growling escalates, take the dogs away from each other with a snap of the leash. Don't pull them away; just like a tight leash, that will make the dogs braver and they are more apt to fight. However, if you snap the leash as you quickly walk away, making the dogs both turn their backs, you distract them and give them a chance to cool off.

If the dogs seem to get along, let them play, dragging their leashes so you can step in if needed. If things start looking too intense, distract the dogs by throwing a ball, calling them to you, or running and playing yourself. It's hard for the dogs to remember why they wanted to fight while they're trying to race the other dog to the tennis ball. Again, interfere as little as possible unless it gets too rough.

To make it easier for your resident dog, your new dog and yourself, you may want to set up two or three meetings between the dogs before you bring your new dog home. After several meetings and playtimes, the new dog will then come home as a playmate and friend instead of a stranger.

Once you bring the new dog home, don't leave the two together unsupervised until you are absolutely positive, with no doubts, that they will get along. Until then, separate the two dogs whenever you leave the house.

Nathan and Jetta

Christy Waehner and her husband Dave adopted Nathan, a former racing Greyhound, from the Greyhound Association of Northern Georgia. Nathan's racing career had been cut short because of an injury. The Waehner's Doberman Pinscher, Jetta, was initially a bit jealous that Nathan had joined the family, but love and affection from her owners reassured Jetta that her place in the family was not threatened, and she quickly learned to accept Nathan.

Christy said of Nathan, "Initially we thought Nathan was on drugs from the track because he was so laid back. I was assured this was not the case and was encouraged to bring him to a lure coursing meet the following weekend. To our surprise, we saw a totally different dog. He came alive! We let him run the course and were awed by his grace and beauty."

"Nathan adjusted quickly to living with us. We let him sleep on the bed and he would stretch out between Dave and I with his head on the pillow. He would snuggle his nose under my neck and let out a long, warm sigh as if this was the best place in all the world."

"Jetta would have liked Nathan to play, but the four-year-old Greyhound had spent his young life working and the concept of play was a mystery to him. All the same, Jetta loved him very

Your Cat at Home

If you have a cat (or cats) at home, it is imperative to ask the rescue group volunteers about your new dog's attitude towards cats before you decide to adopt. Unfortunately, once a dog has learned to chase cats, and especially once it has caught and killed a cat, that dog can never, ever be totally trusted around cats again. That's why if you have cats at home, you must first make sure your new dog is good with cats.

---

much. Together they explored the seashore with us, loved walks in the woods and shared their toys. They were good friends and we loved them both very much."

Jetta and her friend Nathan both passed away in the spring of 1995.

To find a Greyhound adoption group in your area, call Greyhound Pets of America at (800) 366-1472.

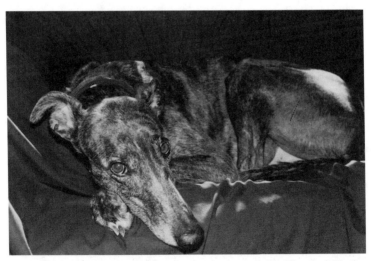

Despite some initial jealousy, Nathan became best friends with the Waehner's Doberman Pinscher. (Courtesy of Christy Waehner)

Contrary to popular belief, cats and dogs can live together peacefully.

Contrary to the old cliché "fighting like cats and dogs," the two species can be friends as long as both are introduced calmly and the dog learns to treat the cat gently and with respect. When you introduce your new dog to your cat, have the dog on a leash and distract the cat by offering some especially tasty treats, perhaps on a saucer on the floor. Endeavor to keep the dog calm. Correct any barking, growling or lunging at the cat. If the cat walks over to investigate the dog, let the two sniff noses but correct the dog should it show any undesirable behavior.

If the cat runs from the dog, the dog will be more likely to want to chase it; that's the prey drive, the instinct to chase moving prey. Even the friendliest of dogs can be a danger to a cat should the cat run. Unfortunately, cats don't know this and their instinct tells them to run. That is why all introductions should be made with the dog on a leash. Then, when the cat runs and your dog tries to chase, you can correct the dog firmly with the leash, offering a verbal correction, "Fido, no! Leave it!" ("Leave it" is a useful command for all sorts of situations, from ignoring the cat to dropping the rotten garbage.)

You may need to supervise interactions between the dog and cat for several weeks. When you can't watch both pets, make sure they are separated. Don't allow them to be together, unsupervised, until you are very, very confidant that the dog won't chase the cat. Remember, the dog only needs to catch the cat once to kill it, or to ensure it forever fears the dog.

However, once the dog and cat learn to trust each other, you'll be pleasantly surprised at the friendships that can develop. For two such different species, they can get along very well.

Your Other Pets at Home

If you share your home with other pets, your new dog will have to learn to live with them, too. Rabbits, ferrets, hamsters, gerbils, reptiles and birds of various sizes, shapes and sounds are all popular pets, and teaching your dog to coexist with them can sometimes be a challenge.

The dog is, by nature, a predator, and small animals such as rabbits and hamsters are prey. The dog must learn to respect, or at least ignore, animals that its instincts tell it to chase and kill. For this reason, your new dog and your other small pets should never be left alone unsupervised. Again, keep your new dog on a leash when you introduce it to your other little pets. If the dog lunges, growls or even looks too interested, correct with a leash snap and "Fido, no! Leave it!"

Rabbits are popular pets and although they are often considered helpless, they can deliver a good kick. However, rabbits will often freeze when frightened and can literally die of stress, so the dog must learn to be quiet and still around the rabbit. If the rabbit is caged outside, the dog could probably be left outside with the caged rabbit without supervision. However, some dogs have been

Champ and Critter

Stan and Sue adopted Champ, a seven-pound Papillon, from the Papillon Rescue League. A day later they adopted Critter, a one-pound ferret, from a local ferret rescue group. Champ had grown up as the only pet of an elderly owner who gave him up for adoption when she needed to move to a care facility. Critter had been in a pet store until the manager decided he was too old to sell.

Champ and Critter, both rescued animals, keep each other active and out of trouble.

known to tear apart the cage to get at the rabbit inside. Be careful and watch to see what your new dog's actions are likely to be before you leave them alone.

Ferrets are very common pets in many areas of the country. These tiny, weasel-like pets are, like dogs, predators by nature. Nothing is quite as cute as a tiny ferret hopping sideways, its backed arched and tail puffed up, chittering away as it tries to get a dog to play with it. Many ferrets have learned to defend themselves by nipping the dog on its tender nose, but a ferret is so small that one bite from the dog could kill it. Again, introduce the two

Stan and Sue closely supervised the first introductions and had both animals on leashes. At their first meeting, Champ tried desperately to ignore Critter, who was bound and determined to get the dog to play. Hopping sideways with his tail puffed up and chittering madly, the ferret would move towards the tiny dog, who would quiver and close his eyes.

However, later that day when Stan was supervising the two animals, Critter grabbed a piece of hair on Champ's tail and pulled. His dignity offended, Champ turned around and barked at the ferret, who hopped and chittered at the dog. Champ play bowed, with his shoulders down and tail wagging wildly in the air. The two dashed back and forth, first Critter chasing, then Champ chasing.

Stan said, "Within minutes they were fast friends, playing gently together, neither trying to hurt the other. After dashing all over the house, they curled up together on the couch and took a long nap. I think that play time was more exercise than either had had in a long time."

Critter is still caged when no one can supervise him, to protect his playmate but also to make sure the sneaky little ferret doesn't get his nose somewhere where it shouldn't be, as ferrets are known to do. But when either Stan or Sue is home and can supervise, Champ will go to Critter's cage and bark, asking his friend to come out and play.

To adopt a Papillon in your area, call the Papillon Club of America's national rescue coordinator at (904) 875-1422.

when the dog is on a leash and correct the dog if it should lunge, growl or snap.

Most ferrets spend most of their day caged and are only out when running around for play time. Most dogs would probably be okay with a caged ferret and would only need supervision when the ferret is out playing.

Birds can be surprisingly delicate, even the bigger macaws and parrots, and because of this, they cannot take much rough handling. Many of the sporting dogs, which were bred to point, flush or retrieve birds, are absolutely fascinated by birds and cannot leave them alone. Even a retriever with a very soft mouth could injure a bird that struggled, and very few birds take kindly to being retrieved by a dog. The larger birds could also hurt the dog, some quite severely. So again, the dog should never be left unsupervised with birds, even with the bird in a cage, as cages are easy to tip over or knock down.

Rats, mice, hamsters and gerbils are all rodents and many breeds of dogs, especially the terriers, were bred to hunt rodents. This instinct can be very strong so it would be wise to protect these little pets from the dog at all times. Make sure their cages are well out of reach.

Lizards and snakes are usually kept in glass terrariums or cages, and these enclosures should be safe from inquisitive dogs. However, when you have your reptile pet out of its cage, watch your dog. Again, these are natural prey, especially for terriers.

Turtles and tortoises often live outside in the backyard and these reptiles can be hurt or killed by your dog. Although it may seem that the animal's shell will protect it, the dog's teeth and jaws are quite powerful and could easily kill the turtle or tortoise. Again, protect this animal from your dog.

Tortoises and lizards should be protected from your dog.

CHAPTER 8

• •

All Dogs Need Some Training

Granite was a handsome Australian Shepherd—jet black with copper and white markings. He had been adopted through the Aussie Rescue & Placement Helpline. His background was unknown and although he seemed to be well-behaved, his new owner thought it would be a good idea for both of them to attend a basic obedience class.

"I haven't had a dog since I was a kid," Granite's new owner said, "and I need to learn what to do. For us, it was the best thing I could have done."

As we saw in Chapter 1, many of the dogs that end up in rescue programs are well-loved pets whose owners cannot keep them, perhaps due to death, divorce or some other legitimate reason. However, vast numbers of dogs are in rescue because of behavior problems. The problems might have been caused by neglectful, ignorant or abusive owners, or because of poor breeding practices that produced a dog with genetic problems. Although training cannot solve all of the problems rescue dogs faced in their old homes, it can help with several problems the dogs and their owners might face in their new homes.

A dog that has come from a good home where it was well-loved and well cared for may grieve when he leaves his old home, but will usually settle into the new home quite well. For this dog and others like him, training can help the dog bond with the new owner and will increase communication between the two so there are fewer misunderstandings.

A dog that has had a less positive start in life may have more difficulty adjusting to her new home and may come complete with behavior problems. She may flinch when you reach towards her and may fear something as simple as a training collar. For these dogs training can be very beneficial, helping the dog learn exactly what is expected. Plus, the interaction between the dog and her new owner during the training sessions will help the bonding process.

Even if your dog had little to no training in her first home, many foster home volunteers start training their charges. If this was the case, the rescue volunteer can tell you what your new dog knows and doesn't know, and what words are used for what actions. For example, was your dog taught to "lie down" or "drop" or "down"?

Training an Adult Dog

Training an adult dog is always different from training a puppy, and training an adult dog with an unknown history can be a challenge. Although the old adage "You can't teach an old dog new tricks" is generally not true, adult dogs have already been exposed to people, many times for the worse, and they are not the clean slates that puppies are. Many times training the adult dog consists more of breaking bad habits than of teaching new things.

Adult dogs may have been exposed to some training; some good, some bad and some awful. One clue that will tell you a little about the dog's previous experiences is his reactions to the training collar. Does the dog stick his head through the collar, wagging his tail, ready to go? His experiences were obviously very positive. Or does he lie down, wagging his tail submissively as he bares his belly? In this case, training was very stressful for him.

Who Is Responsible for the Dog?

When you adopted this dog, was the dog for you? For your kids? For the family? There must be one adult who is ultimately responsible for the dog's care and well-being. Many well-meaning parents want their children to learn responsibility by being in charge of a pet, often a dog. Unfortunately, the majority of children are not able to be fully responsible, and the one who suffers is the dog.

When the question of adopting a dog is being discussed, everyone in the household must get together and realistically discuss the dog's future well-being. Chores can be shared; perhaps Junior will walk the dog daily after school and Daughter will make sure the dog gets a good play time each day. In the morning Dad will feed Rover breakfast and clean up the yard. And then in the evening Mom will make sure Rover is fed again and is groomed.

But even with chores being shared, one person must have the responsibility of making sure everything is done—done completely and done right. Unfortunately, the reality is that on many days Junior will be late, staying at school for football practice, and Daughter may have soccer or band practice. Mom or Dad may have to work late, or go out of town. Someone in the family must have the responsibility of making sure that Rover is cared for properly, no matter what.

If your child forgets to do the dishes, you can let them pile up until there are no clean dishes in the house and the child has learned a lesson about responsibility. But you cannot leave the dog unfed, unwalked, unloved in order to teach your child a lesson, or because it's "not your job."

When it comes to training techniques, there are as many of them as there are trainers and obedience instructors. No one technique or method is right for every dog. Instead, use a method or combination of methods that is comfortable for you and works well for your dog.

In most circumstances, try to use a technique that uses as much positive reinforcement as possible. Although many trainers do use compulsive or force training methods, using these techniques with an adult dog rarely achieves the desired result: a happy, willing, obedient dog. In many instances, using force training methods will only compound already established problems. A frightened dog may become panic-stricken and may try to bite, escape or withdraw into itself. A dominant dog may see forceful training methods as a direct challenge and may try to dominate the owner. Instead, show the dog what to do, teach her a name for that action and reward her when she performs it properly.

The rewards you use should be something that is important to this particular dog. Use a special toy, a happy tone of voice, an ear rub or a scratch on the chest. The positive motivation has to be exactly that: motivational for the dog, so that she is willing to do these things for you.

Unfortunately, your new dog cannot read this and other books and doesn't realize that training would be much simpler if she worked entirely for positive reinforcements. There will be times when you will need to correct your dog. The best correction takes place as the dog makes the mistake and is just forceful enough to get the dog's attention. If your dog is sensitive or fearful, a verbal "Ack! No jump!" may be enough while a less sensitive, emotionally tougher dog may need a collar correction (a snap and release of the collar) along with the verbal correction.

Tailor the correction to your dog. It should be enough to get your dog's attention and no more. Less is better. Then, once the correction is over, show your dog what to do and praise him. For example, if your dog jumps up on you, tell him, "Ack! No jump!" and at the same time, using your hands, shape him into a sit facing you, as you tell him, "Rover, sit. Good boy to sit." As you praise him for sitting, you can pet him. By doing this, you are correcting the undesired behavior (jumping) and showing him what is right (sitting).

Teaching Your Dog

SHOW your dog what to do. Help him into position with your hands, or with a treat or a toy.

TEACH her a word or phase for what you want her to do.

PRAISE him when he does it right, even when you help him.

Do not correct her until she **UNDERSTANDS** what you are expecting her to do.

When correcting him, use only as much **FORCE** as needed and no more. Less is better.

TIMING is everything; praise her as she does something right and correct her as she makes a mistake.

Be **CONSISTENT** and be **FAIR.**

Teaching an alternative action also works very well. Teaching the dog to sit, for example, also teaches the dog not to jump on people. Or, as another example, when your new dog comes trotting down the hall with your leather shoe, take that away as you tell her, "Ack! No!" then hand her one of her toys, "Here. This is yours. Good girl!"

The Basic Commands

All dogs need to know a few basic obedience commands. These commands allow you not only to control your dog's actions so that you can ensure his safety, but also to help the dog live comfortably with you. The training techniques listed below work for most dogs. However, because each dog is an individual and reacts to training differently, an alternative training method might be needed for your dog. If you're having problems, call a professional dog trainer or obedience instructor for help.

Sit. As we already mentioned, when you teach your new dog to sit, she cannot jump on you at the same time. If the dog sits when guests come over, she cannot jump on your guests. By teaching your dog to sit for everything she wants—petting, treats, toys or meals—you can eliminate many jumping problems.

To teach your new dog to sit, hold his leash close to the collar with your left hand. With your dog in front of you, hold a treat or toy in your right hand and move it up over his head and back towards his tail as you tell him, "Rover, sit." Your dog will sit because he cannot continue to stand and look at the treat disappearing over his head. When he does sit, praise him, "Good boy to sit!"

To help your dog learn to sit, hold his collar . . .

. . . and gently tuck him into a sitting position.

If you find that Rover will not hold still and starts to spin as you move the treat, or if the treat is not a motivation to your dog, then gently shape him into the sitting position: With your dog by your left side, hold the front of your dog's collar with your right hand and use the left hand to slide down the dog's back to his hips, tucking him into a sitting position. Tell him, "Rover, sit," as you shape him into position.

When you're ready for your dog to move from the sit (or any other position you teach) tell him, "Rover, okay!" which means, "You can move now, we're done with that command."

The sit will work if you teach your dog that he must sit each and every time you say it. And say it only once. The command is "Rover, sit." Not, "Rover, sit. Sit! SITSITSITSIT!"

Tell him once to sit and then use your hands to put him in position. When he learns that good things happen when he sits, he'll come running to you, sliding into a sit in front of you. And then you will, of course, praise him enthusiastically for doing so!

Lie Down. The lie down command teaches your dog to lie down and be still. It doesn't mean lie down and crawl, or thrash, or roll. It means lie down and be still.

To teach the down, start with your dog in a sit, preferably by your left side. With a treat or toy in your right hand, let your dog smell it, then take it straight to the ground in front of her paws. When she starts to follow the treat down, you can put your left hand on her shoulders to help her. When she lies down, give her the treat and praise her, "Good girl to lie down!"

If your dog won't follow your hand with the treat, shape her into position by scooping her front legs out and down. Start with her in a sit, and as you tell her, "Ginger, lie down," gently pull her front legs forward and down, using your left hand to put gentle pressure on her shoulders to encourage her to lie down.

Again, as with the sit, tell your dog, "Ginger, okay!" when you're ready for her to get up and move. Remember, you decide when the command is finished, not your dog.

To teach the down, start with your dog in a sit with a treat or toy in your hand. Let your dog smell it, then take it straight to the ground in front of her paws. She'll follow the treat down.

Stay is taught with your dog either sitting or down. Use both a verbal command, "stay" . . .

Stay. The stay command will be used with both the sit and the down commands. You want your dog to understand that stay means, "Hold this position until I tell you to move." Because holding still is hard for most dogs, teach it very gradually, asking your dog to hold still for just seconds at first.

The stay is taught using both a verbal command ("stay") and a hand signal (a wave of the hand with the open palm toward the dog). Both commands should be given at the same time.

With your dog in either a sit or a down, on leash, give the stay commands and take one step away from the dog, holding the leash. Be quiet, don't praise him right now, and don't repeat the stay command. Count to five slowly, then go back to your dog and praise him. If, while you're counting to five, your dog moves from the position, tell him, "Ack! No!" put him back into the position where you left him and repeat the stay command.

. . . and a hand signal—a wave of the hand with the open palm toward the dog. Both commands should be given at the same time.

Don't be in a hurry to increase the time or distance away from your dog. It will take time, repetition and patience. Increase the time and distance very gradually. As your dog is learning this command, always practice it with his leash on.

The stay has many practical applications around the house. Tell your dog to sit-stay when you open a door; this teaches him not to dash out the door. Have your dog do a down-stay when you're eating; this keeps him from begging under the table. Have him do a down-stay when company comes over so he's not jumping all over your guests. Let them pet him only when he does a sit-stay. As you teach the stay, use the leash to control your dog's actions; you don't want him to dash away from you when you tell him to stay.

As your dog learns to stay, increase your distance very gradually.

Come. This is your dog's most important command. Not only is life much easier with a dog who comes when she's called instead of you having to chase her, but more important, responding to this command promptly can save your dog's life.

One easy way to teach this command is to teach your dog what the box of treats sounds like. Shake the box of treats, pop one in her mouth and praise her. When she starts running directly to you when she hears the box of treats, start saying, "Ginger, come!" as you shake the box. This teaches her that coming to you brings positive results.

You also need to teach the come command when your dog is on leash. Although the come with treats teaches your dog that coming to you is fun, she also needs to learn to come to you each and every time you call her. On the leash, if she decides to make a detour or to ignore you, you can use the leash to make her come to you.

As you are teaching this command, never, ever call your dog and then punish her. That's guaranteed to teach her to run the other direction when you call her. If she had an accident in the house or chewed up your sofa, go get her.

Heel. The traditional position for a dog walking with you is at your left side, with the dog's neck and shoulders by your left leg.

Fuzzy Finds a Family

Kim Martin adopted Fuzzy, an Alaskan Malamute, from the Georgia Alaskan Malamute Rescue group. Fuzzy was six months old when she was adopted and had already been diagnosed with hip dysplasia.

Kim and Fuzzy bonded almost immediately. "Fuzzy is one of the most wonderful things to come into my life. Being a military wife whose husband is assigned to a rapid deployment unit, I'm alone a lot. When I got Fuzzy, I found I wasn't alone anymore; I had a friend and companion. In fact, she's my best friend, my protector and a playmate. Fuzzy likes to do silly things that make me laugh. She gives me as much love as I give her, if not more.

"Fuzzy was an abused dog and when I first got her she was afraid of men or anyone carrying something in their hands. But all my neighbors were understanding and soon she was the favorite dog of the neighborhood. All the kids come to play with her.

"She is now an integral part of a loving family who treasures her and will be there for her when her hips go bad. She knows that she is loved and will always have a home with us."

To find an Alaskan Malamute recsue group in your area, call Alaskan Malamute Protection League at (505) 281-3961.

In this position, your dog can watch you and can walk with you, turning when you turn, slowing or speeding up with you as you change pace.

Most dogs pull their owners down the street because they are paying attention not to their owners, but to everything else. An out of control dog can be both dangerous and in danger. Going for a walk is much more enjoyable when the dog is under control and is walking nicely with you.

Bring a treat or toy up towards your face as you say, "Watch me."

Don't forget the praise when she does!

The first part of the heel exercise is teaching your dog to pay attention to you. With your dog in front of you, show him a toy or treat and tell him, "Watch me!" as you take the treat up to your chin. As your dog's eyes follow your hand up, praise him as he looks at your face. "Good to watch me!"

When he will look at you easily just standing or sitting in front of you, you will want to teach him that he can pay attention to you as he's walking. Tell him to watch you and then start walking backwards. Encourage him to follow you. If he looks away or starts to sniff the grass, tell him, "Ack! No! Watch me!" When he looks back up at you, praise him.

When you can back away from him and keep his attention, you can start teaching the heel. Have your dog sit by your left side and tell him to watch you. When you have his attention, start walking forward as you tell him, "Rover, heel!" If he continues to pay attention to you, praise him. If he starts to pull forward or sniff the grass, back away from him quickly as you tell him, "Rover, watch me!" Back away a few more steps, get his attention back on you and start all over again.

Practice this in short increments. Heel for six feet, stop, have Rover sit and praise him. Do it again, just for six feet. Gradually extend it to 10 feet, then 15. Then add turns to the left and right, as well as about turns. Walk fast, slow and in between. Keep your training sessions short, sweet and exciting.

When to Call for Help

Remember that when you are training a recently adopted dog, you are dealing with the unknown. A dog's past has a tremendous bearing on her future and it's difficult to decipher from a dog's bearing exactly what has happened to her in the past.

A dog can be, just by her very nature, a dangerous animal. She can bite, often severely. If at any time during the adjustment period or during training you feel ill at ease with your dog, or afraid, or if you simply have questions, ask for help. Call the rescue group, your veterinarian, or the trainer or obedience instructor you talked to when you adopted your dog. Remember, it's their job to help you, so let them!

CHAPTER 9

● ●

Have Fun With Your Dog!

If you and your dog enjoy training and cherish your time spent together, check out some of these activities and see what strikes your fancy. With most of these sports, you can use the activity as a training challenge, as good, plain fun or as a competitive sport.

To compete in American Kennel Club (AKC) or United Kennel Club (UKC) events, your dog must be registered with the sponsoring group. However, if your dog didn't come complete with registration papers (most rescue dogs don't) don't worry—you can still participate. The AKC and UKC issue what are called Indefinite Listing Privilege (ILP) papers. These allow your dog to be recognized as a member of its breed for competition only in performance events. To obtain an ILP application, write to the organization you would like to compete under (addresses are in the Resource Section at the end of this chapter).

A few of the activities, like search and rescue or therapy work, are not sports at all but are, instead, serious, worthwhile, rewarding careers. So read on, and see what looks good to you. A Resource Guide at the end of this chapter will help you find out more about these activities. And have fun with your dog!

Agility

Agility is an active sport that is a combination of a child's playground, a grand prix jumping course (like that for horses) and a law enforcement dog obstacle course. Your dog must run through tunnels, leap over jumps of different heights and shapes and climb over obstacles.

Agility training helps develop your dog's body awareness; the dog learns where his feet are and how to know where to step, jump or climb. The dog also becomes more aware of his balance. A dog involved in Agility training gains confidence, too, both in himself and his abilities and in you, as his trainer—you will make sure the dog doesn't hurt himself, that he can succeed and that you both will have fun.

Agility training is also good for you, as your dog's trainer. You learn how to communicate with your dog, showing him what you

Agility builds athleticism and confidence in a dog.

want him to do. After all, your dog has no idea why you want him to jump through a tire when it's so much easier to go around!

Agility competition does require a physically fit dog and owner. To compete, your dog will also need obedience training so you have good, reliable off-leash control.

The one drawback to Agility is that it does require equipment. However, if you have the space and the skills, you can build your own. If that is unrealistic, many dog training clubs and training schools now have Agility equipment.

If you and your dog enjoy Agility training, you can earn Agility titles in competition. The American Kennel Club offers a Novice Agility Dog (NAD) title, an Open Agility Dog (OAD) title, an Agility Dog Excellent (ADX) and a Master Agility Excellent (MAX). The United States Dog Agility Association offers the titles of Agility Dog, Advanced Agility Dog and Master Agility Dog.

Canine Good Citizen

The AKC began the Canine Good Citizen program in hopes of combating some of the negative publicity that dogs have had recently. The AKC wanted to show the general public (and the media) that there are a lot of good dogs and responsible owners in local communities that are not normally in the media spotlight simply because they aren't in trouble. Bad news *is* news! However, the AKC wants to promote good dogs and good owners and is doing so by establishing and promoting this program and by helping community clubs and dog trainers publicize the Canine Good Citizen tests.

The Canine Good Citizen (CGC) program is open to all dogs, registered and nonregistered, purebred or mixed breed. The dog and owner take a short test, which does require some previous training. In the test, the dog must allow a stranger to approach the dog and the owner. The stranger will shake hands with you and greet your dog. The dog should sit by your side and not move, should not jump on the stranger, growl, bark or misbehave in any other way. The dog must also allow someone to touch him, pet and groom him. The dog again must remain in the sitting position by your side and should not show any shyness or resentment.

You and your dog must also demonstrate that the dog will walk on a leash without pulling, even in a crowd situation, do a sit on command, a down and stay, and come when called. Your dog will then be subject to several distractions, including another dog, a loud sound such as a book being dropped and a jogger dashing past.

The last part of the test is supervised isolation. You will tie your dog and, leaving her under the judge's supervision, go out of sight for five minutes. Your dog should not bark, whine, pace or howl.

At the successful completion of the test, the dog is awarded a certificate that states she is a Canine Good Citizen and is entitled to use the initials "CGC" after her name. The test is given by dog training clubs and dog trainers and is sometimes given at dog matches. If a local dog trainer does not offer the tests, write to the AKC for information about someone in your area who does.

Carting

Carting and draft dogs have been used by dog owners for thousands of years. Dogs have pulled sleds, wagons and travois, carrying or pulling home the results of a hunt, household furnishings, people or supplies. In many parts of the world horses, oxen or other large beasts of burden were not available or practical for these tasks, but dogs were.

Today, carting can be a fun sport with competitions much like driving horses, or it can be a practical skill, helping you around the house or yard. When you go shopping and bring home a 40-pound bag of dog food, hook your dog up to his wagon and let him bring in his food. When the trash cans have to go out to the end of the driveway, load them in your dog's wagon. Dogs love to work, especially for the people they love.

Dogs at Work

Some very special rescue dogs can be trained and placed in working homes. Tippy became a service dog after an Obedience career and motherhood. When her original owner was killed in a car crash, Tippy was trained to assist a woman who had been severely injured in a car accident. She learned to turn light switches on and off, to retrieve dropped items, to pull the wheelchair, to steady her owner when she got into and out of the wheelchair and much, much more.

Some dogs end up doing very special jobs for others.

Tom Bradley also lives a much fuller life because of a rescue dog. Tom was injured in a diving accident and is now a quadriplegic. His partner, Thunder, retrieves household items identified by name, pulls his wheelchair, gives him plenty of love and affection, and has even protected him from an intruder. Tom calls Thunder his best friend.

• Many larger dogs are serving as guide dogs for the blind and
• service dogs for the disabled. Hearing alert dogs for the hearing
• impaired come in any size, shape or breed. Rescue groups or
• breeders that have promising dogs needing homes can contact
• training organizations that provide dogs for the disabled.

Flyball

Flyball is a team relay sport. Each team consists of four dogs and four owners. The dogs, one at a time, run and jump over a series of hurdles and then step on the lever of a box that throws a tennis ball. When the dog catches the ball, she turns around and runs and jumps over the hurdles again, bringing the ball back to you, at which time the next dog starts. The team that finishes first wins.

Flyball is a lot of fun, especially for dogs that are tennis ball crazy. However, it does require some equipment. You will need four hurdles per team, plus one flyball box per team. And of course, you need dogs and owners for your team, as well as for competing teams.

The North American Flyball Association offers three titles for Flyball competition: Flyball Dog (FD), Flyball Excellent (FDX) and Flyball Champion (FDCh). All are earned on a point system.

Frisbee

Frisbees are almost as popular with dogs as they are with people. Chasing a flying disc that swerves, climbs, banks and otherwise tantalizes the dog is even more fun than a tennis ball.

If your dog is enthused about chasing a Frisbee, she can play for fun and exercise to use up some of that excess energy or she can chase a Frisbee in competition. Each year, communities throughout the country sponsor local competitions for

Frisbee-catching canines. The dogs chase the flying discs, leap incredible heights to catch it and then chase it again. Regional competitions follow the community competitions and the winners go on to the World Finals.

Eldon McIntire and his Australian Shepherd, Hyper Hank, were pioneers in the sport. McIntire and Hyper Hank performed their Frisbee magic at National Football League halftime shows, including an exhibition at Super Bowl XII.

Hiking and Camping

Do you like to go for walks in the country? Do you love the smell of a meadow in bloom in the spring? Or the smell of a pine forest after a rain? Is a weekend walk a good stress reliever for you after a hard week at work? If so, then take your dog with you when you walk. The American Dog Packing Association is made up of dogs and owners who like to go hiking with their dogs. Some take day hikes, others go camping, backpacking and hiking.

Hiking is not competitive. However it is great exercise and, when shared with friends, is a great social activity. Short hikes, gradually increasing in length or difficulty, can help you and your dog get back into shape if you have both been couch potatoes. As your dog gets more fit, she can start wearing a dog pack, carrying water, first aid supplies and treats.

Scent Hurdles

Scent hurdle racing is much like flyball, except that after your dog races over the hurdles, he must then use his nose and find a dumbbell that has your scent on it. Once your dog finds the correct dumbbell, he has to pick up the dumbbell and return over the hurdles to you.

Again, like flyball, scent hurdle racing is a team sport, with four dogs and owners. The first team to finish wins.

Contact your local dog trainer or dog training club to see if they have a team, or if they would be interested in starting a team.

Schutzhund

The sport of Schutzhund is German and was originally used to test military and law enforcement dogs, as well as working dogs, for suitability for breeding. In the United States, Schutzhund is a competitive sport combining obedience, tracking and protection. As your dog competes at various levels, she can earn titles, including Sch I, II and III. In addition, there are tests for endurance, traffic safety, drafting, companion dogs and watchdogs. Titles are available in each area of competition.

Some Schutzhund clubs allow only the traditional German working dogs to compete: German Shepherds, Rottweilers and Doberman Pinschers. Other clubs allow any dog capable of doing the work.

Any dog that participates in Schutzhund training must be of sound, stable temperament and must be physically fit. You, as the trainer, must take this training seriously. A protection or attack trained dog is not a plaything, but instead, is a potentially dangerous weapon.

Search and Rescue

Search and rescue work is extremely rewarding. There is nothing like the feeling you get when you and your dog find a small child lost in the woods or an elderly man who wandered away from a nursing home. Search and rescue dogs have worked the San Francisco, Mexico City, Armenia and Los Angeles earthquakes, the Oklahoma City bombing, as well as flood emergencies, collapsed buildings and mud slides.

Search and rescue work is also extremely demanding. It requires a lot of training—sometimes as much as a year or two, depending upon the level of training you and your dog have before you start. You will need to know map reading, orienteering, wilderness survival, emergency first aid and much more. Your dog will need to learn how to use its nose, both for air scenting and tracking, and must be able to alert you when it has found a scent.

You and your dog both will have to be in good physical condition before you are able to search effectively. Your dog will also need obedience training, especially good off-leash control.

Skijoring and Sledding

Skijoring has been around for centuries in Northern Europe and probably originated when a cross-country skier hooked up a reindeer and allowed the animal to pull him along. Horses have been used for skijoring for a number of years in both Europe and North America, and it was only natural that eventually a dog would be used to pull the skier—after all, not everyone can keep reindeer, caribou or horses.

When people think of sled dog racing, they traditionally think of the Alaskan tundra and a half-frozen musher on a sled pulled by half-wild Huskies traversing miles upon miles of frozen wasteland. Sled dog racing, however, can be for anyone with a sled and a team of dogs that like to run. Some of the different teams have included Standard Poodles and Irish Setters.

Sledding can also be a fun way to exercise your dog. When my husband and I lived in Virginia, the neighborhood kids would come knocking on the door every morning after a snowfall, asking if the dogs could come out and play. They would hook up each dog to a sled or saucer and have races. The dogs and kids both loved it.

Therapy Dogs

Ursa has an instinct for knowing who needs her, and during visits to nursing homes or Alzheimer's care facilities she will go directly to that person, sitting quietly by their side, nudging their hand until they pet her. She will allow kids to pull her ears, sit on her, climb all over her or cry into her coat. Her love and affection, given without reservation, have helped numerous people.

We, as dog owners, know that our dogs are good for us. They are good for us physically, mentally and emotionally. Only recently have researchers come to the same conclusion, and out of this knowledge has emerged therapy dogs. Therapy dogs can help many people: the emotionally distraught, the mentally ill, abused children, orphaned or runaway kids, the sick, the elderly, the disabled and the lonely.

Therapy dogs like this Landseer Newfoundland provide love and affection without making demands.

Researchers have not been able to pinpoint exactly why or how therapy dogs help people, but they do have some guesses. First of all, therapy dogs provide love and affection without making demands: The dogs simply give love. The dogs are nonjudgmental; they don't care what people look like, how much money they have or what ethnic background they come from. And finally, the dogs make people smile. Laughter is good for our soul and dogs love to make us laugh.

A therapy dog must be well trained, with a good foundation in the basic obedience commands, especially sit, lie down and stay. The dogs cannot jump on people nor can they paw or scratch at people. During the specialized training for therapy dog work, the dog must be exposed to a variety of sights, sounds and smells that he will face in a nursing home, hospital or day care center. That might include strollers, wheelchairs or gurneys, respirators, urine bags and diapers. The dog must be able to climb stairs, use an elevator and an escalator.

Many therapy dogs are taught specialized behaviors that can make their work easier, including putting their front feet up on the arm of a wheelchair or on the side of the bed and turning around so people in a chair or in bed can reach to pet them. Many therapy dog owners also teach their dog tricks to amuse the people they are visiting.

Tracking

Tracking is an activity that allows the dog to use his natural ability to smell. You can use tracking as a recreational sport, teaching your dog to "Go find Dad" or "Go find the kids," or you can use it as a competitive sport, earning tracking titles through the AKC, the Australian Shepherd Club of America (yes, they offer competition for all breeds!) or through a Schutzhund club. Tracking skills can also be used with a search and rescue group.

Resource Guide

Agility

For information about the location of Agility training clubs and Agility competition, write to the AKC at 5580 Centerview Drive, Raleigh, NC 27606 or to the U.S. Dog Agility Association, P.O. Box 850955, Richardson, TX 75085-0955.

The North American Dog Agility Council (NADAC) also offers competition and titles, and may be reached at HCR 2

Box 277, St. Maries, ID 83861. The Trans-National Club for Dog Agility is located at 401 Bluemont Circle, Manhattan, KS 66502-4531.

Some good books are *Enjoying Dog Agility—From Backyard to Competition* by Julie Daniels (Doral Publishing, New York, 1990) and *Agility Training: The Fun Sport for All Dogs* by Jane Simmons-Moake (Howell Book House, New York, 1991).

Canine Good Citizen

For more information about training for the Canine Good Citizen test, look for *The Canine Good Citizen: Every Dog Can Be One* by Jack and Wendy Volhard (Howell Book House, 1994).

Copies of the test rules can be obtained from the American Kennel Club.

Carting

For more information about carting, try *Cart and Sled Dog Training* by Raymond Thompson, 15815 2nd Pl. West, Lynwood, WA 98036; or the carting information packet put out by the Newfoundland Club of America (your dog need not be a Newfoundland), NCA Land Work Secretary Roger Powell, 5208 Olive Rd., Raleigh, NC 27606.

You can also write to *Dog Fancy* magazine (P.O. Box 6050, Mission Viejo, CA 92690) asking for the August 1988 issue. On page 65, the article "Putting the Dog Before the Cart" will help you train your dog. *Dog World* magazine (29 N. Wacker, Chicago, IL 60606) has an article "Carting From A to Z" in its May 1992 issue that is also very helpful.

Flyball

For more information, write to the North American Flyball Association, 1 Gooch Park Dr., Barrie, Ontario, Canada L4M 4S6.

A good book to look for is *Flyball Racing* by Lonnie Olsen (Howell Book House, New York, 1997).

Dog Fancy magazine (the address is above) also had an article on page 32 of its August 1990 issue titled "Flyball" that will tell you more about the sport.

Frisbee

If you would like more information about Frisbee competition, call Friskies Canine Frisbee Championships at (818) 780-4915 or (800) 423-3268.

For training tips, look for Karen Pryor's book *How to Teach Your Dog to Play Frisbee* (Simon & Schuster, New York, 1985).

Dog World magazine (the address is above) has an article in its January 1986 issue on page 10, "Frisbee—From A to Z" that will help you teach your dog to play the game.

Hiking and Camping

For more information on hiking with your dog, write to The American Dog Packing Association, 2154 Woodlyn Rd., Pasadena, CA 91104.

Some good books are *Backpacking With Your Dog* by Charlene G. LaBelle (Alpine Publications, Loveland, CO, 1993), and *On the Trail With Your Canine Companion* by Cheryl S. Smith (Howell Book House, New York, 1996).

Schutzhund

For more information, write to Landersverband DVG America, 113 Vickie Drive, Del City, OK 73115; or United Schutzhund Clubs of America, 3704 Lemoy Ferry Rd., St. Louis, MO 63125.

Ask at your library or bookstore for *Schutzhund* by Susan Barwig and Stewart Hilliard (Howell Book House, New York, 1991) or *Training the Competitive Working Dog* by Tom Rose and Gary Patterson (Giblaut Publishing, Colorado, 1985)

Dog Fancy magazine (the address is above) had an article in its June 1990 issue on page 60, "Schutzhund Training," which explains the sport and training in greater detail.

Search and Rescue

For more information, write the National Association for Search and Rescue, P.O. Box 3709, Fairfax, VA 22308; or SAR Dog Alert, P.O. Box 39, Somerset, CA 95684.

A good book on the subject is *Search and Rescue Dogs* by the American Rescue Dog Association (Howell Book House, New York, 1991).

Skijoring and Sledding

For more information about skijoring and sledding, write to the International Federation of Sled Dog Sports, 1763 Indian Valley Road, Novato, CA 94947; or the International Sled Dog Racing Association, P.O. Box 446, Norman, ID 83848-0446.

You might want to read *The Joy of Running Sled Dogs* by Noel Flanders (Alpine Publications, Loveland, CO, 1988). Raymond Thompson Co. (the address is above) also offers two books: *Novice Sled Dog Training* and *Skijoring With Dogs*.

Therapy Dogs

For more information, there are several therapy dog organizations: Love on a Leash Therapy Dogs, 3809 Plaza Dr., No 107-309, Oceanside, CA 92056; Delta Society Pet Partners Program, P.O. Box 1080, Renton, WA 98057; Therapy Dogs International, 6 Hilltop Rd., Mendham, NJ 07945; Therapy Dogs Inc., P.O. Box 2786, Cheyenne, WY 82003.

Volunteering With Your Pet by Mary R. Burch, Ph.D. (Howell Book House, New York, 1996) will give you a detailed description of how you and your dog can get involved in therapy work.

Another good book is *Therapy Dogs: Training Your Dog to Reach Others* by Kathy Diamond Davis (Howell Book House, New York, 1992).

Tracking

Write to the AKC or the Australian Shepherd Club of America at 6091 East State Highway 21, Bryan, TX 77808-9652, (409) 778-1082 for copies of the rules and guidelines for their tracking competitions.

For more information about tracking, ask at your library or bookstore for *Tracking Dog: Theory and Methods* by Glen Johnson (Arner Publications, Canastota, NY, 1975), or *Training the Competitive Working Dog* by Tom Rose and Gary Patterson (Giblaut Publishing, Colorado, 1985).

• •

CHAPTER 10

Working Through Problem Behavior

Very few dogs are intentionally bad. When your dog digs up your nicely landscaped backyard, he's not saying to himself, "Ha! I'll get even with her for going to work every day and leaving me here at home alone!" Even though you might believe he's muttering this under his breath, he's not. Revenge is a totally alien concept to dogs.

Unfortunately, many dogs are given up by their owners because of behavior problems. Your new dog might have been given up because she likes to chew on things, or bark or dig. But just because your dog's first owner wasn't able to deal with those problems doesn't mean they are unsolvable. You also don't know how much effort the first owner put into solving the problems, and you have no idea how much the first owner actually *caused* the problems.

Changing Problem Behavior

Most dogs don't get enough exercise. When your dog has energy to spare it has to be expressed in some manner, and many times your dog will use that energy to amuse herself. That might be by destroying your spa cover, chewing up the chaise lounge cushions or uprooting all your rose bushes. When she's doing this, she's not thinking about what will happen when you come home eight hours later; she's simply using up energy and having fun. Regular strenuous exercise can use up some of that energy more constructively.

Nutrition also plays a part in problem behavior. A dog with a poor diet that's hard to digest may crave certain vitamins or minerals, or may simply be hungry. These dogs often chew on inappropriate things such as dirt, rocks, plants or the stucco on the house. Feed a top-quality food, and if you think your dog may have a nutritional deficiency of some kind, talk to your veterinarian.

Play can also be a problem-solver. Life is not all work; play is vital to good emotional health. Play is especially important to help relieve stress, and rescue dogs have experienced plenty of stress, so make sure you take the time to play with your dog. Throw the ball, make goofy faces or just lie on the floor and tickle your dog Laugh with her. You'll be amazed at how much better you'll both feel.

As we've mentioned before, dogs are creatures of habit and a routine makes your dog feel secure. This routine is very important when your dog is getting to know you and your household, but even later when he's settled into your family, routine gives him security. Try, whenever possible, to feed him at the same time each day, to walk, train, exercise and spend time with him at specific times.

Regular training should be part of your dog's routine. Your training sessions teach your dog much more than sit, down, stay and come. These sessions also teach your dog to work for you. When you remember that almost all of the breeds of dogs in existence today were bred to do a job, you can see that work is very important to a dog. A positive training program also reinforces in your dog's mind that you are the leader.

It's also important for you to remember that although chewing, digging, barking and jumping on people are problems as far as you're concerned, they're not problems to your dog. These are all very natural behaviors. He digs because he smells a gopher or because he wants to lay in the cool dirt during hot weather. He barks because he's bored, or hears a noise, or hears a siren. He

Training Rules for You

Before you begin training, keep these rules in mind:

1. Don't scream and shout at your dog; she can hear you just fine.

2. Never train your dog when you're sick, angry, drunk or stoned. You will be inconsistent, your judgment will be impaired and your dog won't understand you.

3. Be consistent with your rules.

4. Keep the training sessions short and sweet.

5. Always, *always* end your training sessions on a high note.

6. Be patient.

chews because he's teething or because it's fun. And so on. We consider them problems because we don't like them, and although we can strive to change these behaviors we must keep in mind they are natural. We must have realistic expectations.

Destroying Your Yard

You cannot correct problem behavior that you cannot see (or hear) happen. If your new dog likes to dig up your grass and garden, leaving giant craters all over the yard, or if your dog likes to chew or tear up your plants, you cannot correct her when you get home eight hours later. You may think that by correcting her then your dog will understand, but she won't. She may understand that you are upset about the hole in the back yard, but she won't connect that with the act of digging it eight hours ago. Instead, she will learn to dread your coming home because that's when she gets into trouble. And tomorrow, when she starts to dig again, the correction you gave when you came home won't have any relevance at all until it's time for you to come home again; then she'll start to get anxious.

Head off digging problems in the yard by giving your dog her own fenced in dog run.

Instead, you must set up a situation so that you can correct her when you are at home and prevent the problem from happening when you cannot supervise her. By preventing the problem you can either stop it from turning into a habit, or if it's already a habit you can break the cycle.

Preventing it from happening might mean that you need to build your dog a run. A run is a fenced in area that is totally your dog's; here he can dig and play to his heart's content. This is his area. Make it safe for him, putting away anything that might be dangerous and making sure he has shade somewhere in the run all day. Have an unspillable water container and leave him a few toys. Put a radio in the window overlooking the run and turn it to an easy listening station before you leave each day. After all, music does soothe the savage beast!

If there are some existing holes in your yard, fill them in with gravel, rocks or your dog's feces. This will make the holes much less attractive for your dog to dig up again. If she's digging near the fence, fill the holes with larger rocks or even garage sale bowling balls. These are very difficult for the dog to move and will discourage her from trying to get under the fence.

Some garden problems start when your dog sees you gardening. Your dog sees you dig, play with the plants and even hide things in the dirt. When you go inside the house, the dog wanders over to investigate and before you know it, all your flower bulbs have been dug up and deposited on your back porch. You're upset but your dog just thinks its a fun new game!

If you like to garden, either put your dog in the house while you're gardening, fence off the garden or distract your dog by giving her a new chew toy.

Your dog needs to be taught what is acceptable and what is unwanted. That means you must prevent the problem from happening when you are not there to watch him, and then when you are at home observe him as much as possible, praising him for good behavior and correcting him when he starts to get into trouble.

Destroying Your House

The dog that destroys the house needs to be treated much like the dog that destroys the yard. Allow your dog freedom of the house only when you can supervise him, and then keep him in the same room with you. When he's quiet, chewing on his own toys, praise him. When he picks up something he shouldn't, correct him and hand him one of his toys. Don't let him sneak off to another room.

When you're not at home, put her in her kennel crate (see Chapter 6) or put her outside in her run. Destructiveness can be caused, or made worse by lack of exercise, boredom or loneliness. Keeping your dog stimulated and happy will go a long way toward eliminating her destructiveness.

Nuisance Barking

Several years ago at a mayoral conference, a survey of the nation's mayors listed barking dogs as one of the major complaints received by the mayors' offices, right behind crime and drugs. Barking dogs can be a nuisance, interrupting sleep and creating gigantic rifts in your relations with your neighbors.

No Quick Fixes

Many dog owners go to a training class or hire a trainer because they want some (or all!) of their dog's problem behaviors "fixed." It's not that easy. Usually problem behaviors are a combination of things, both yours, your family's and your dog's. One of the primary causes of behavior problems occurs when your dog does not accept you as the leader of his pack. He may look upon you as a friend or a buddy, but unless he sees you as his leader he really has little reason do follow your instructions.

Other things can also contribute to problem behavior: lack of exercise, poor nutrition, external factors (the neighbor's kids) and so on. You need to look seriously at your dog's environment and make whatever adjustments are needed.

1.   You, as the leader of the pack, *always* eat first.

2.   You *always* go through doors first and up stairs first. Make the dog wait until you give permission.

3.   Have his bed (kennel crate) next to yours and have him sleep there, with the door closed.

4.   Feed her a good quality food, preferably meat-based instead of soy- or grain-based. Pay attention to the additives, preservatives and colorings. You don't want her eating too much junk. Feed in the morning and the evening, putting the food down for 15 minutes, then taking away any leftovers. Don't leave it out all day.

5.   Make sure he gets good, strenuous exercise *every* day.

6.   Practice your obedience training daily. Don't skip a day. And use your training in your daily routine, making Ginger sit for treats, petting, and so on.

7. Have your dog do down-stays in the house with you close by. Have her down-stay while you watch your favorite sit-com or the news on television. Have her down-stay while you eat dinner.

8. Don't pet your dog too much. The leader, or dominant dog, *doesn't* fawn over subordinates. (But do make sure to schedule some petting and hugging during the day.)

9. Don't play games that teach him to use his strength against you—tug of war, wrestling or fighting. Instead, play retrieving games, or hide and seek games; constructive instead of combative games.

10. It's your house. Your dog is living in your house with you, not visa versa. You can set the rules and you can tell your dog that he must abide by them.

Your dog might bark because he's bored, lonely, hears other dogs barking, hears a siren or an alarm, or even because he has an over-developed sense of protectiveness. You can teach your dog not to bark when you're home by interrupting the barking with a correction, "Rover, quiet!" and then praising him when he is quiet, "Good boy to be quiet!"

If your dog doesn't stop for a verbal correction, don't yell louder. That will only make him think that he's right for barking because now you're barking, too! Instead, use a squirt bottle with plain water, or water with a touch of vinegar, and squirt him with it as you tell him to be quiet. When he stops barking, backs up and tries to lick the vinegar off his muzzle, tell him how good he is to be quiet.

You should never leave your dog outside all night, whether he barks or not. It is not safe or healthy for the dog.

Teaching your dog to sit for petting will stop him from jumping on people.

Jumping on People

Dogs jump on people to greet them face to face—after all, that's how puppies greet adult dogs. We don't like big dogs to jump up on people because their nails are sharp and can scratch people and rip clothes, and because a big dog can knock someone over. Teaching your dog to sit for everything, including petting, will go a long way towards stopping the jumping problem. After all, your dog can't sit and jump on people at the same time.

If your dog is very excitable you may have to correct him for jumping until he understands that he must sit. There are a couple of different ways that you can do this. First, to correct your dog from jumping on other people, use the leash. Out in public use the leash to control your dog and, if you need to, your hands to make him sit (one hand on his collar and one on his hips). Don't let

When Your Dog's Heart Has Been Broken

Dogs bond with people; that's what they are supposed to do and what they have done for thousands of years. And unfortunately, dogs don't screen the people they bond with. As a result, many times—in fact, too many times—people will break their dog's heart. People will often give up a dog just as easily as they acquired it, with no thought of the poor dog, who loved his owners more than they loved him. The dog tied in a barren backyard loves his people, even if he only sees them minutes each day. Dogs even love abusive owners—after all, they are still the dog's people.

However, once a dog's heart has been broken, for whatever the reason, that hurt will remain. It is part of her and will, at some point, affect her relationship with you. She may be worried when you sweep the floor or yell at the kids. She may cling to your side like a second shadow or she may pace and whine when you leave her home alone. Some rescue volunteers even compare it to post-traumatic stress disorder.

That doesn't mean the relationship won't work, though. You will need to be patient, kind and considerate but you will still need to be your dog's leader. Bond with him, play with him, train him, exercise him and keep him on a regular schedule. And most of all, love him.

people pet him until he's sitting, and if he's too excited ask people to ignore him until he's calmer.

In your home, leash your dog before you let guests come inside. If you need to, you can call out to people, "I'll be right there. Let me leash the dog!" Then, once the dog is leashed, you can let your guests in. Again, you can ask your guests not to pet your dog until she's under control and sitting.

To keep your dog from jumping up on you, you can grab her collar as she jumps up and tell her, "Ack! No jump! Sit," and make her sit, using your hands if you need to. Don't praise or greet her until she's sitting. In the beginning, you may need to keep your hands on her to make sure she doesn't jump up and bash you in the face with her head as you're bending over her.

The key to correcting a jumping problem is consistency. You must make your dog sit all the time, not just at certain times or when you're wearing certain clothes. Make him sit for petting *all* the time. Don't let guests or friends tell you, "Oh, it's okay. I don't mind if he jumps." Your dog cannot second-guess who to jump up on and who not to, so make him sit all the time.

Patience and Understanding

When you understand why your dog does what she does, and if you are patient about teaching her, your dog will have an easier time changing her behavior. Your dog can learn to live by your rules as long as you are very clear about your rules, communicate what is right and what is wrong, and are consistent about enforcing those rules.

We have shared this world with dogs for over 20,000 years, and throughout that time there have been compromises on both sides. With compromises and patience, it can be a wonderful relationship.

CHAPTER 11

• •

When It Just Isn't Working

Not every dog is right for every person, and not every person is right for every dog. Sometimes two personalities just don't mesh well or perhaps, for whatever reason, the relationship is full of hurt, anger or mistrust. If you adopt a dog and find that after a reasonable period of time it just isn't working, you may have to send the dog back to the rescue group.

What is a reasonable period of time? You might have known as soon as you brought the dog home that this just wasn't the dog for you. Maybe the dog tried to eat your cats or growled at your children. Maybe you knew within a week or so that your household was too loud, too active and too rowdy for the quiet dog you brought home.

Unfortunately, sometimes it takes longer to realize that a situation just isn't going to work. When you have taken the time to try to bond with the dog, have spent quiet time with him, played with him, exercised and started training him, and you just know deep down in your heart that this isn't going to work—for whatever reason—then call the rescue group and let them know.

There's nothing to be ashamed of in admitting that this placement didn't work. After all, you can't share your home with just any person, can you? The relationship between a dog and his owner is just as personal in its own way.

Whatever you do, don't be ashamed of calling the rescue group back. Even if you do feel embarrassed, don't turn the dog over to someone else. Almost all rescue groups have in their adoption contracts a statement that you must call them if you cannot keep the dog. Some groups will go to great lengths to enforce that contract, including legal action.

When you do call the rescue group, be honest about why you can't keep the dog. Don't make excuses. If the dog is aggressive toward cats, tell them. They can then try to place the dog in a home without cats and they can notify the new owner that the

---

Black Baron Finds His Home

Baron was neglected in his first home. The majestic black German Shepherd had been bought as a status symbol—something to show off—and had then been ignored. After being rescued from that home by German Shepherd Rescue, Baron was adopted by a woman who already had a German Shepherd and wanted another. However, she soon realized that she wasn't capable of handling the big dog and she gave him back to the rescue group. Black Baron, who by then was distrustful and wary of people, was then adopted by Bob Stout, a dog trainer who saw the intelligence and nobility of the dog and understood just what he needed.

Bob, who lived alone, quickly taught Baron the basic obedience commands and found the dog a willing and eager student. Within a few months Baron was working on and off leash, was following hand signals and was even pulling a wagon. "I was getting tired of carrying firewood," Bob said. "So I bought a used dog wagon and taught Baron to pull it. Now I can load the wagon with firewood and make one trip instead of several."

Over the years, Bob and Baron's life changed. Bob married and three other dogs arrived to share Baron's home. When the children were born, Baron accepted them, too, and was very tolerant of their poking fingers and clumsy steps. In fact, the children's bedroom became his favorite place in the house.

dog is not to be trusted with cats. If the dog growls at kids, they can then reevaluate the dog's personality and temperament and decide whether or not he is even safe to adopt out.

In Chapter 1 we saw that many people give dogs up for frivolous reasons, but there are valid reasons why someone can't keep a dog. The death of the dog's owner, an owner's move to a care facility or a military transfer overseas can all be legitimate reasons to give up a dog. Again, when you must give up your adopted dog, even if it is many years later, call the rescue group.

As Baron grew older, his muzzle started to show gray and his steps slowed, but the noble look in his eyes remained. The intelligent dog who was once tied to a tree outside the home of an uncaring owner finished his life as a loved and loving companion.

Black Baron had several owners before he found the one who understood him.

What Will Happen to Your Dog?

In most cases, if the dog is still of good temperament and can still pass the evaluation process, she will be found another home. Just because you and the dog might not be right for each other doesn't mean the right person isn't out there somewhere waiting for that dog—they are, just as there is a dog out there waiting for you.

Just because this adoption didn't work out, don't give up. Go through the screening process again, using what you have learned about this situation. Why didn't this work? Was it the dog's activity level? Personality? Breed? Attitude? Something else? Take this information and incorporate it into your selection process. And then try again.

If you must give up the dog for other reasons, such as an overseas move or because you must move to a care facility, your dog will go through the evaluation process again and, depending upon the rescue group, your dog will probably be placed in a foster home until an adoptive home is found.

What happens if your dog doesn't pass the evaluation process? That depends upon the rescue group involved. Some will call you back and ask what you would like done. Sometimes volunteers with a rescue group take in and keep unplaceable dogs. Other groups will euthanize a potentially dangerous dog or an unadoptable dog. Some groups have a "no-kill" policy and will find a placement for the dog in a long-term care shelter or kennel. If you're concerned about what will happen, talk to the rescue group volunteer and ask.

. . . .

PART III

Your Dog's Health

• •

CHAPTER 12

Caring for Your Dog

Caring for your dog properly encompasses body and coat care, nutrition, exercise, play and training, as well as the dog's emotional well-being. All of these things require a commitment of time and effort from you, but are amply rewarded by your dog's good health and companionship.

The easiest way to make sure your dog is well cared for is to set up a routine and write it down, either on a sheet of paper posted on the refrigerator or on a bulletin board. If more than one person is involved in the dog's care, have people check off the items as they are completed. Once the routine is established, follow it. It's too easy to say, "Oh, I'll do that tomorrow." But proper care of your dog is not something that can be put off.

Be patient with your dog as you initiate her routine. She may not have been handled much in her first home; perhaps no one ever cleaned her ears or brushed her teeth. All of these things may be new to her and, because of this, might be frightening. As you introduce brushing, combing, ear and teeth cleaning, and so on, do so gradually and with lots of sweet talk. Try to keep force to a minimum and instead, show her that caring for her is a positive experience. Follow up your grooming and care session by giving her a treat or a chance to chase her ball.

Daily Care Routine

Once a day you need to run your hands over your dog, getting to know the feel of him, checking for ticks, burrs, foxtails, lumps, bumps, bruises, cuts and scrapes. As you do this each day, your fingers will get to know the feel of the dog and you will learn what feels normal and what doesn't. By doing this, you will be able to catch a little problem before it turns into a much bigger problem.

To give your dog a body exam, sit down on the floor and lay your dog on his side. Starting at his nose, run your hands over his muzzle and head. Get to know the shape of his head so you will be able to feel a bump or bruise or swollen lymph glands. Lift up your dog's lips and check his mouth. The gums should be firm; if they are swollen, the dog might have some debris that needs to be cleaned out or there might be an infection. His eyes should be bright and clear with no discharge. Any dry matter (or sleep matter) should be wiped away with a clean cotton ball.

Lift up each ear flap and check inside each ear. If the dog has an infection, the inside of the ear will smell bad and there will be a dark discharge or a buildup of wax. Run your fingers around each ear where it attaches to the head—sometimes ticks lodge themselves there. A tick will feel like a small to large bump under your fingers. The next chapter discusses how to remove a tick from your dog.

You might also find tangles of hair behind the ears or behind and between the back legs. Called mats, these can be combed out or very carefully trimmed out with rounded scissors. Mats can occasionally be found in the longer hair on the back legs also, especially if a burr is in the hair and has started a tangle.

Continue your massage, working down your dog's neck and shoulders. Run your hands down each front leg, encircling the leg, checking the elbow for cuts and the armpit for ticks. Check the paw for burrs or foxtails lodged between the pads or cuts and scrapes. Burrs and foxtails (grass seeds) can become imbedded, which is very painful, and can work themselves into the skin, causing an abscess.

Check each toenail. It's not necessary to trim the nails daily, but check the nail to make sure it's not broken. If it's rough or broken, you can trim it with a pair of nail clippers made for dogs or file it with an emery board or nail file. Don't use your nail clippers, as they will squeeze the nail and possibly split it.

After finishing the front feet, continue your examination of the dog's body, running your hands around the rib cage, down the back to the hips. Check the genital area. It's important you know what is normal and what is not, so if your dog has a genital discharge or swelling you will recognize it as different and call your veterinarian. Check the tummy, including the nipples. Feel for lumps or bumps.

Check for fleas. If fleas are a problem in your area and if your dog has any, you will see them on the tummy. To get rid of fleas, you need to get them off your dog by bathing or spraying and you need to treat your house and the yard. Just doing one of these things will not take care of all the fleas. And you will need to repeat the entire process, sometimes monthly throughout the summer. Fleas are survivors! (For more on removing fleas, see the next chapter.)

Continue your examination of your dog by checking his back legs and feet just as you did the front legs. Finish by checking the tail and the anal area. If the dog has had soft stools there might be evidence on her coat, in which case you will need to find out why. Did someone sneak the dog some scraps and upset her stomach?

Once you and your dog get the hang of this exam and you know what is normal and what is not, this will take you about 10 minutes. Don't try to rush it. If you do, you may miss something important. Instead, take the time to do it thoroughly and spend at least 10 minutes going over the dog. Then, once you have examined the dog, you can finish the exam by giving her a body massage. Your dog will totally relax and you both will enjoy it.

A side benefit of this exercise will show up when you need to take your dog to the veterinarian. Because your dog will be so used to being handled, if the vet needs to look in her ears or check her teeth, the exam will be easy and won't be as traumatic as if the dog weren't handled thoroughly every day.

Feeding Your Dog

There aren't many subjects that evoke such strong feelings as does a discussion about dog food. Some dog owners are adamant about feeding a specific brand, others swear by a certain type of food or ingredient. There is a reason for these strong feelings: Other than genetics, the heritage your dog received from its parents, good nutrition is probably the single most important factor responsible for your dog's continued good physical and emotional health.

A dog fed a poor food or a food he cannot adequately digest will have dull eyes and a poor coat, will lack energy and stamina and will not be able to work well. In addition, the dog may have food related allergies and can, over time, develop other health problems, including thyroid deficiencies, skin diseases, stomach and intestinal gas, rickets, bloat and a variety of other problems.

Dry food is recommended over canned dog foods because it has a good shelf life, is easily stored and provides good exercise for the teeth and gums. Canned foods are much more expensive and, although they are very palatable to most dogs, they do not provide the good chewing action that can help keep the teeth clean. Semi-moist foods are also very palatable but many are preserved with sugar, an ingredient most dogs are better off without, and, like canned foods, do not provide any chewing exercise.

There are some very good dog foods on the market whose makers are conscientiously trying to produce a good, healthy product. Natural Life is a wonderful food with no chemical preservatives. Nature's Recipe offers a variety of foods, including a lamb and rice kibble with no by-products. Solid Gold is an all natural kibble that is recommended for dogs with skin problems. Generations of dogs have grown up on Science Diet dog foods. Iams is another brand that has been around for years and has a wonderful reputation.

There are also foods for every stage in the dog's life: puppy, adult, maintenance, gestation and lactation, performance, diet, senior, even foods for allergic or ill dogs. These foods vary by protein or fat content, ingredients, digestibility and more. If you have questions about what food you should feed, call your veterinarian or the dog food manufacturer. Keep in mind while shopping and reading labels, as with many other things in life, cheaper is not necessarily better. The better quality dog foods will be more expensive. However, what they save you by giving you a healthier dog with lower vet bills is more than worth it.

If you are trying to control the amount of salt or fat your family eats, you understand the importance of reading labels while grocery shopping. It's the same with dog food. The label on the package of your dog's food will tell you, in decreasing order, the ingredients found in a particular food, as well as the protein, fat, fiber and water content. It's important you know and understand what the label says and what is actually in the food you are feeding your dog.

Most dogs need meat in their diet. Scientifically classified as carnivores, meat is the mainstay of wild canines, although all will, if given the chance, eat fruits, berries and greens.

The meat used in dog food does not have to meet the standards set for human consumption, which means just about any part of the animal can be included. An ingredient listed as "beef" does not mean ground round; instead it might be ears or muzzles, beef scraps or other cuts not considered fit for human consumption. An ingredient listed as "meat" or "meat meal" can be just about anything that comes off an animal, including hide, hooves and meat scraps, and when listed as such, is usually a compilation of different kinds of animals. If it was only beef, it would be listed as beef.

Keep in mind, however, that when a wild canine kills to eat, it usually eats the entire animal, including the skin and some of the fur, the entrails, the smaller bones, the marrow in the larger bones, the organs, even the food being digested in the prey's intestinal tract.

Beware of the phrase "by-products" on the label. If the label reads "chicken by-products" that does not mean scraps of chicken meat—it means heads, feet, bills, bones, even feathers. It can even mean waste products, diseased animals or tumors. If that makes you sick, it should. Instead of feeding a food that lists by-products, look for a food that lists a specific meat, such as beef, chicken or turkey.

Other ingredients that can add protein to the food might include dairy products, cheese, whey or eggs. This protein, whether from meat, eggs or dairy, is necessary for growth, for developing strong muscles, bones and teeth, for healthy organs and coat and actually, for life itself. However, more is not better. Although puppies usually need a higher protein content in their food (24 to 26 percent is usually recommended), adults require far less. Dog foods are available with a protein content of over 30 percent, but digesting and metabolizing these diets can actually do your dog more harm than good. Talk to your veterinarian about how much protein he or she recommends for your dog.

All dry kibble foods will also include a grain product, either wheat, soybeans, rice, barley or corn or a combination of several. These carbohydrates are sources of energy. The cellulose found in plants aids in the absorption of water and in the formation and elimination of stools.

Label readers are used to looking at the fat content of food. We know we should reduce our fat intake, although some fat is necessary, for us and for our dogs. Fat soluble vitamins require fat to be used in the body. Fat helps maintain a healthy hair coat and alleviates dry skin and is also the most concentrated source of energy in times of hard work or stress. Fats also increase the palatability of food. Many of the dry dog foods advertised as "natural" foods use fats as a preservative. This can reduce the amount of chemicals contained in the food, but often these foods have a reduced shelf life. If you decide to feed your dog a dry food preserved with fat, just make sure the food is not rancid.

When choosing a food, read the list of ingredients carefully, look at the percentages of protein, fat, fiber and water and then use your common sense. Does this sound good to you? If you have any uncertainties, talk to your veterinarian or call the dog food manufacturer. Most manufacturers have a telephone number listed on the label. Ask them how the food is manufactured and tested. Ask them about quality control or ingredients. They will, of course, try to sell you their food, but calling them is a good way to get your questions answered.

Some dogs have food allergies and scratch themselves raw if they eat wheat, while others have terrible intestinal gas if they eat soy. You might be able to identify food allergies simply by trial and error. However, your veterinarian can do an allergy test, similar to those used with people, to identify allergy causing foods. You can then eliminate those from your dog's diet. There are many special diets available commercially that your veterinarian can tell you about.

Most experts agree a good quality commercial dog food contains, nutritionally, everything a dog needs. However, most dog owners add supplements to their dog's food, for a variety of reasons, and most dog food manufacturers confirm that as long as the supplements do not exceed 10 percent of the food fed, they probably will not disturb the nutritional balance of the food. Of course, this depends on what is being fed and what is being supplemented.

Many dog owners add yogurt to their dog's food. Yogurt has been said to aid digestion by adding beneficial bacteria to the intestinal tract. Yogurt is nutritious, is a good source of fat and certainly will not hurt the dog, as long as your dog has no allergies to dairy products.

Brewer's yeast is another common supplement. Many dog owners believe dogs who eat brewer's yeast will naturally repel fleas. This has never been proven scientifically, even though many dog owners adamantly believe in it. As with yogurt, yeast is an excellent food (providing B vitamins) and will not hurt the dog when used as a supplement.

Many dog owners who take vitamins themselves give their dogs a multivitamin and mineral supplement. Again, this will not hurt the dog as long as it is given according to directions.

However, more is not better. Too much calcium can cause serious problems in puppies and growing dogs, as can zinc. Although water-soluble vitamins (such as vitamin C) can be excreted through the urine, fat-soluble vitamins (such as vitamin A) will build up in the body and can actually become toxic if over-supplemented.

Vegetables, vegetable juice or meat broth can be added to your dog's dry food. The vegetables add nutrition while the broth can make a dry food more palatable. Cooked eggs can be added as a nutritional supplement or to make the dry food more attractive, as can cheese or cottage cheese. A carrot makes a good chew treat and a slice of apple is a much better sweet treat than a commercial treat containing sugar and artificial colors.

Some dog owners, frustrated over the quality of ingredients available in commercial dog foods, cook their own dog food. Others feel it is easier to control what their dog eats when they prepare the food. If your dog has a food allergy, feeding a homemade diet will make it easier to keep her away from foods that cause problems. If you do cook for your dog at home, you will need to take care she is being fed a quality, balanced diet.

The following is a basic diet that would be suitable for most dogs. Working dogs might need more, as would gestating or lactating bitches. A sedentary house dog would need less.

Cook one and a third cups of raw brown rice. Mix with one cup of browned meat (ground beef, ground chicken or turkey, with grease drained off), a half cup of chopped or shredded vegetables (carrots, green beans, peas or broccoli; cooked or raw) plus two tablespoons of bone meal, a dash of iodized salt, a teaspoon of vegetable oil and a heaping tablespoon of yogurt with active, live cultures. Top it off with a good vitamin and mineral supplement.

You can vary this diet by replacing the rice with boiled or baked potatoes, by adding lentils or cooked kidney beans in place of the other veggies, or by using cooked eggs or cheese in place of part of the meat.

Keep in mind no one food is totally nutritionally complete and while hamburger and rice, with supplements, is okay for a few meals, it would be deficient over a longer time. It's important when cooking a homemade diet that you pay particular attention to supplying your dog with a balanced diet, varying the ingredients and paying close attention to your dog's health. At the first sign of a dull coat, excessive shedding, poor stools or any other change in the dog's health, talk to your veterinarian.

Once you have chosen a food, introduce it to your dog gradually. If you change over a period of three weeks—feeding 25 percent new food and 75 percent old food the first week, half new and half old the second week, and 75 percent new and 25 percent old the third week—your dog's system will have a chance to adjust. If you abruptly change foods, your dog will almost certainly have an upset stomach and diarrhea.

Regulate how much to feed your dog by how he looks and feels. If the dog is thin and is always acting hungry, give him some more food. If the dog is fat, cut back. Along the same lines, if he has been working hard give him some extra, and if he has just been lying around cut back.

When you feed your dog, don't leave food available all the time. Not only will this draw ants and other unwelcome freeloaders, but your dog will think food is always available. It's more important that your dog learns food comes from you. In a pack situation, the leader always eats first and gets the choicest food. In your family pack, you will always eat first and then you will feed your dog. When your dog is through, take away her bowl. If your dog plays with her food or walks away without finishing it, after 15 minutes pick up the bowl anyway. Don't give your dog anything else to eat until it's time for the next meal.

Water is as important as food for your dog. Water is necessary for life and your dog should have access several times a day to fresh, *clean* water. Although drinking out of the toilet bowl seems to be a natural for many dogs, never let your dog drink out of the toilet if you use the type of toilet cleaner that releases a small amount of cleaner each time the toilet is flushed; many of these cleaners are toxic. Even if you don't use such a cleaner, never let your dog drink from the bowl right after you've cleaned it; traces of the cleaners may still be in the water.

Your dog must have ample time to go outside to relieve himself. As an adult, your dog will probably have one to two bowel movements per day. The bowel movement should be solid and firm enough to hold together. A soft stool could be caused by diet, medications, stress or disease. If your dog has a stool that contains mucus or has blood in it, or a worm segment, save a piece of the stool in a plastic bag and call your veterinarian.

Pick up your dog's feces daily. Accumulated stools will spread disease or parasites, will smell and will attract flies. When out in public with your dog, always carry a plastic bag so that you can pick up any stool your dog might leave behind.

Your dog will also urinate several times a day. The frequency will depend upon how much the dog drinks, the size of her bladder and her individual preference. If the urine appears very dark, smells especially strong or appears to have blood in it, call your veterinarian right away.

Weekly Care

In addition to her daily exam, your dog also needs some weekly care. You can set aside a longer session once a week, or you can do one of these tasks each day.

Once a week, during your dog's daily care routine, you need to clean her teeth. There are several different ways to do this and many products on the market to help you. One of the easiest ways to keep your dog's teeth healthy, clean and looking good is to use gauze and baking soda. Wrap a couple of layers of wet gauze around your index finger, dip it into some baking soda and rub it back and forth over your dog's teeth. Use the baking soda liberally and let it sit on the dog's teeth for a few minutes before allowing the dog to drink. The baking soda will help guard against plaque buildup, and if your dog eats dry food and regularly chews on rawhides or hard toys, his teeth should remain healthy longer.

If your dog already has some plaque built up, you may need help from your veterinarian to clean it off. Then you can keep up on the routine care.

Toenails also need weekly attention. Many active dogs will wear their toenails down, but if your dog runs on dirt or grass his nails may need to be trimmed. Long nails are more than simply unsightly, they can actually deform the foot, arching the toes unnaturally and causing pain.

If your dog has any white nails, you can see the pink quick and you will be able to trim the nails without causing the quick to bleed. If your dog's nails are black, you can usually trim the hook at the end without trouble. However, if you are uncertain, use a nail file to file the nails shorter or ask a dog groomer or your veterinarian to show you how to safely trim the nails.

Once a week you also need to gently wipe the inside of your dog's ears using a cotton ball moistened with either alcohol, witch hazel or a product made especially for cleaning the ears. Clean only where your finger can easily move. Do not put your finger or a cotton swab into the ear canal.

A healthy ear will smell slightly damp and may have some dirt and wax residue but will not need more than one or two cotton balls to clean it out. If the ear smells bad (foul or dirty) and it takes several cotton balls to clean it, then it's time to call your veterinarian because your dog may have an ear infection. If your dog is shaking his head a lot, or is pawing or scratching at his ears, he may have a foxtail in his ear or might be starting an infection. Ear problems can sometimes be difficult to clear up and are very painful, so don't procrastinate getting your dog in to see the veterinarian.

If you check your dog's body daily for burrs and foxtails, she can get by with one thorough brushing a week, although two or three times a week is better, especially in the spring and fall when the dog is shedding.

You may want to lay your dog down on the floor to brush her, as you do when you check over her body and massage her. Start brushing at the head, working through the ruff (around the neck), brushing in the direction the coat grows. If you part the coat with one hand and brush with the other, you can get through the thickest coat. A wire or stiff bristle brush will help you get through the coat to the skin. Work around the neck and down to the shoulders, down the back, to the hips. Go back up to the neck and work down the chest, down the belly to the pantaloons (the hair on the back of the legs.)

Then go back over your dog, brushing against the coat, loosening all the dead undercoat. Finish by running a comb over the

Patricia and Bailey

Patricia Mills of Oceanside, California, adopted Bailey, a handsome brown and black brindle Greyhound, from Greyhound Pets of America. This organization rescues former racing Greyhounds who might otherwise be destroyed.

Bailey became part of Patricia's family in November 1991. He was nervous and shy at first and leery of strangers. Although in good health, he had not yet been neutered. Patricia and Bailey attended a basic obedience class and with training, love and affection, he is now a much more confident dog, although he is still shy with strangers.

However, when he meets people he knows he is almost wild with joy. Patricia said several of their neighbors have become his special friends and he eagerly solicits their petting.

Bailey is also a couch potato, Patricia said. "Bailey's couch is *his* couch. If someone happens to sit on it, he doesn't know what to do. He looks at them, walks around the couch and then looks at me. He's plainly confused."

Patricia says Bailey is a wonderful addition to her family. "I have enjoyed watching his personality blossom. He is a dear, sweet dog."

dog, again in the direction the hair grows. When you are done, there should be no tangles and you should be able to run your fingers through the coat. It should feel like silk.

If your dog has a short coat, it still needs to be brushed. Use a soft-bristled brush and follow the same directions as above, except that you will not have as much coat to work with.

You will need to decide how often your dog needs to be bathed. If she is a working therapy dog she will need to be bathed weekly or before each visit, and because of this you will need to use a very gentle shampoo that won't dry out her coat and skin. If your dog lives in the house at night and works hard on the farm during the day, she may need to be hosed off daily and shampooed

To find a local Greyhound rescue group, call Greyhound Pets of America at (800) 366-1472.

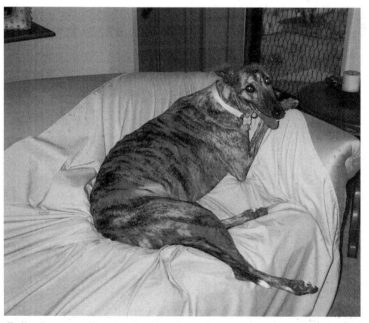

Bailey has gone from racing Greyhound to couch potato. (Courtesy of Patricia Mills)

every other week. Or maybe she will need to be bathed once a month, depending on your schedule. It's up to you.

You may want to trim the hair around your dog's anal area, especially if it gets dirty. You will also want to keep the hair on the feet trimmed. Using a pair of rounded tip scissors, simply trim the hair between the pads and around the nails.

Annual Vaccinations

The rescue group probably started your dog on a vaccination schedule that you continued with your veterinarian. The commonly given vaccinations include distemper, hepatitis, leptospirosis, parvovirus, corona virus and rabies. Depending upon where you live, your veterinarian might also recommend a Lyme disease vaccine.

Vaccines are either killed or modified live forms of the actual virus. When injected, the vaccine stimulates your dog's immune system to produce antibodies, so if your dog is exposed to the disease his body will fight it off and he won't get sick. All of these diseases can rapidly kill unvaccinated puppies, healthy adult dogs and occasionally, as with rabies, even people. Chapter 13 discusses these diseases in more detail.

The advent of these vaccinations has saved millions of dogs' lives over the past few decades and it's vitally important that you keep track of your dog's vaccinations and get yearly boosters. If you have any questions about what vaccines your dog should have, talk to your veterinarian.

Identifying Your Dog

If your dog were to get out of your yard, do you have any means of making sure he would be returned to you? Is your dog identified, beyond a shadow of a doubt, so you can identify him to someone else? If there are three tri-colored Shetland Sheepdogs at your local Humane Society, how could you prove to the officer in charge that your dog is yours?

The first way to identify your dog is with a collar and tags. The collar should be a buckle or quick-release collar. Don't leave a choke or slip collar on your dog all the time, because it could get caught in a bush or on the fence and choke and kill your dog. The tags should include your dog's license, a rabies tag and an identification tag with your address and telephone number. When you go on vacation, let your dog wear a temporary tag with your hotel number or the campground written on it.

Although it is important that your dog wear a buckle collar with identification tags, collars can come off. Your dog also needs permanent identification. A tattoo, usually placed on the inside of the right rear leg, can be a permanent form of identification. Most people use their Social Security number because it is a one-of-a-kind number, assigned to no one else but you. Other numbers include the dog's AKC registration number, your driver's license number, a spouse's birthday or your winning lottery numbers.

The numbers used are not as important as the fact they are registered with the National Dog Registry, an organization whose sole function is to maintain a list of dog tattoos and notify owners when the dog has been found. The National Dog Registry's telephone number is (914) 679-2355. They also maintain a list of people who can tattoo your dog for you.

Many rescue groups will not release a dog to its new owner without first microchipping the dog. A microchip is tiny, about the size of a grain of rice, and is programmed with a unique code. The microchip is injected by a veterinarian under the dog's skin between the shoulder blades. When a scanner is passed over the dog's shoulders, the microchip sends out the code, which the scanner reads.

Like a tattoo, the number must be registered somewhere, along with information about the dog's owner. There are several such registries, and their fees vary. The HomeAgain Companion Animal Retrieval System is operated by the American Kennel

Club, although its registration services are open to all companion animals. The owner of the pet fills out a registration form, and this information goes into a database with nationwide 24-hour access. For more information, write to the American Kennel Club, Companion Animal Recovery, 5580 Centerview Drive, Suite 250, Raleigh, NC 27606-3394 or call (800) 252-7894.

Another 24-hour registry service is operated by InfoPET. You can write to them at 415 W. Travelers Trail, Burnsville, MN 55337 or call (800) INFO-PET.

PETtrac is a national registry for pets implanted with the Avid microchip. For more information, call (800) 336-AVID.

CHAPTER 13

Safeguarding Your Dog's Health

The best safeguard for your dog's health is to develop a working relationship with a veterinarian you trust. Talk to the vet about your dog, his health now and anything you know about his past health. Tell your vet about your dog's activity level and behavior. And then listen to your vet's responses. Ask questions. If your vet is threatened by your questions, find another vet. This is your dog, your companion, and it's up to you to make sure he lives a long, healthy, happy life.

Infectious Diseases

Many of the diseases discussed below can often be prevented by vaccinations. However, vaccinating your dog is no guarantee that she will not get sick. There are many factors that govern how a dog reacts to a vaccine, including the antibodies the puppy got from her mother, how the dog's own immune system reacts to the vaccine and her general state of health. Set up a vaccination schedule with your veterinarian and stick to it, making sure your dog completes her vaccination schedule and gets her boosters. If you suspect your dog has any of these diseases, take her to a veterinarian immediately.

Distemper is a very contagious viral disease that used to kill thousands of dogs. With the advent of new, effective vaccinations, it should not kill any dogs today, but unfortunately, it still does.

Dogs with distemper have a fever, are weak and depressed, have a discharge from the eyes and nose, cough, vomit and have diarrhea. An infected dog sheds viruses in its saliva, urine and feces. Intravenous fluids and antibiotics may help support an infected dog, but unfortunately, most infected dogs die.

A distemper vaccination can normally prevent distemper. However, vaccines work by stimulating the immune system. If there is a problem with the immune system or if your dog has not received a complete series of vaccinations, he may not be adequately protected.

Infectious Canine Hepatitis is a highly contagious virus that primarily attacks the liver, but can also cause severe kidney damage. It is not related to the form of hepatitis that infects people. The virus is spread through contaminated saliva, mucus, urine or feces. Initial symptoms include depression, vomiting, abdominal pain, high fever and jaundice.

Mild cases may be treated with intravenous fluids, antibiotics and even blood transfusions, but the mortality rate is very high. Vaccinations, usually combined with the distemper vaccine, can prevent hepatitis.

Coronavirus is rarely fatal to adult dogs, although it is frequently fatal to puppies. The symptoms include vomiting, loss of appetite and a yellowish, watery stool that might contain mucus or blood. The stools carry the shed virus, which is highly contagious.

Fluid or electrolyte therapy can alleviate the dehydration associated with diarrhea, but there is no treatment for the virus itself. There is a vaccine available, sometimes given alone, sometimes given with the distemper, hepatitis, leptospirosis and parvo vaccinations.

Parvovirus, or parvo as it is commonly known, is a terrible killer of puppies. A severe gastrointestinal virus, parvo attacks the inner lining of the intestines, causing bloody diarrhea with a very distinctive odor. In puppies under 10 weeks of age the virus attacks the heart, causing death, often with no other symptoms.

The inflammation of the intestinal lining (called gastroenteritis) can be treated with fluid therapy and antibiotics. However, the virus moves rapidly and dehydration can lead to shock and death in a matter of hours. There is a vaccination for parvo, which is often given combined with the distemper, hepatitis, leptospirosis and corona vaccines, although some experts believe it should be given alone.

Leptospirosis is a bacterial disease. The disease is spread by infected wildlife, the bacteria being shed in the urine. When your dog sniffs at a bush that has been urinated on, or drinks from a contaminated stream, she may pick up the bacteria. The bacteria then attack the kidneys, causing kidney failure. Unfortunately, people can also pick up lepto.

Symptoms of lepto include fever, loss of appetite, possible diarrhea and jaundice. Antibiotics can be used to treat the disease, but the outcome is usually not good due to the serious kidney and liver damage caused by the bacteria.

Care must also be taken not to spread this highly contagious disease to other dogs, animals and people. Dogs do receive a vaccination for lepto, usually included with the distemper, hepatitis, parvo and corona vaccines.

Tracheobronchitis, commonly called kennel cough or canine cough, is a respiratory infection that can be caused by any number of different viral or bacterial agents. These highly contagious, airborne agents can cause a variety of symptoms, including inflammation of the trachea, bronchi and lungs as well as mild to severe coughing. Antibiotics may be prescribed to combat or prevent pneumonia and a cough suppressant may quiet the cough.

Some forms of the disease, such as *Bordetella bronchiseptica* and canine adenovirus, may be prevented by vaccination, but there are so many causes that vaccinations alone cannot prevent tracheobronchitis.

Rabies is a highly infectious virus usually carried by wildlife, especially by bats, raccoons and skunks, although any warm-blooded animal, including humans, may become infected. The virus is transmitted in saliva, through a bite or break in the skin. The virus then travels up to the brain and spinal cord and throughout the body.

Behavior changes are the first symptom of rabies. Nocturnal animals come out during the day, fearful or shy animals become bold and aggressive, or friendly and affectionate. As the disease progresses, the animal will have trouble swallowing and will drool or salivate excessively because of nerve paralysis. As the disease progresses further, paralysis and convulsions develop.

There is no effective treatment for rabies; however, vaccinations are very effective.

External Parasites

Fleas are small insects, each about the size of the head of a pin. They are crescent shaped, have six legs and are spectacular jumpers. Fleas live by biting their host animal and drinking its blood.

You can tell if your dog has fleas by brushing back his coat and looking at the skin. A flea will appear as a tiny darting speck, trying to hide in the hair. Roll your dog over and check his belly, near the genitals—any fleas will be scurrying to hide. You can also tell by laying your dog on a solid-colored sheet and brushing vigorously. If you see salt and pepper type residue falling onto the sheet, your dog has fleas! The residue is made up of fecal matter (the "pepper") and flea eggs (the "salt").

A heavy infestation of fleas can actually kill an animal, bleeding it dry. Keep in mind each time a flea bites, it eats a drop of blood. Multiply that by several bites a day (or more!), times the number of fleas on the animal.

The flea, biting its host, can also cause innumerable skin problems. Many dogs develop flea allergy dermatitis, a reaction to the flea bite. The bite causes a never-ending cycle of self destruction:

the flea bites, the skin itches, the dog scratches or chews in response, the skin becomes even more irritated, so the dog bites or chews even more. Pretty soon the dog is miserable and needs veterinary care.

Fleas can also carry disease. Rats and the fleas that bit them carried bubonic plague in Europe and Asia during the terrible Medieval epidemics. Fleas are also the intermediary host for tapeworms. If you have found small, rice-like segments near your dog's rectum or in her stools, your dog has tapeworms.

To reduce the flea population, you need to treat the dog and the environment. If you simply treat your dog and do not treat the yard, house or car, your dog will constantly become reinfected. If your dog is working on a ranch and it's not possible (or desirable) to constantly use insecticides, then you will have to concentrate on keeping the dog itself flea-free.

Fleas, ticks and all kinds of internal parasites can lurk in your yard. That's why you need to protect your dog with regular exams.

There are a number of different products on the market, including strong chemical insecticides, natural botanical products and a systemic birth control pill you give your dog that stops the fleas' reproduction. What you decide to use depends upon how bad your flea problem is and your preferences. The stronger chemicals, such as organophosphates and carbamates, will kill the fleas, of course, but they can also kill local birds and wildlife. You must take care that you use them properly.

The natural products are not as strong and some of them do not kill the insect immediately; sometimes it takes a few hours. Some of the natural products use silica or diatomaceous earth to cut or erode the flea's shell so that it dehydrates. There are also natural products that use citrus oils, eucalyptus or pennyroyal oils to repel fleas.

Many of the older systemic products were mildly toxic to dogs, but the newer ones are not, and represent a great advance in flea control. Ask your veterinarian about a flea control product called Program. This is a monthly pill given to your dog that acts as birth control for the fleas, interrupting their reproduction. It is very effective and is harmless to both dogs and humans.

If you have any questions about what is safe to use on your dog, call your veterinarian or your groomer. If you have questions as to how to use a particular product, call the manufacturer. They will be more than willing to talk to you and explain exactly how their product should be used. Great survivors, flea eggs can live in the environment for years, waiting for the right conditions to hatch; this is not an insect that can be ignored!

Ticks are another insect that cannot be ignored. There are several different kinds of ticks, all roundish insects that bury their head in the skin of the host animal. They feed on the host's blood and, when full and engorged, drop off.

Unfortunately, ticks can be very dangerous and can carry several potentially deadly diseases. Rocky mountain spotted fever is carried by the infectious agent *Rickettsia rickettsii,* a parasite that lives in ticks. Dogs that get rocky mountain spotted fever run a fever of 104 degrees or higher, become listless and depressed, don't eat, have swollen lymph glands and often have difficulty breathing.

When people get the disease, the symptoms include fever, headache and a rash. Rocky mountain spotted fever can be accurately diagnosed by blood test, and aggressive treatment with antibiotics is required to clear it up.

Lyme disease was first reported in Lyme, Connecticut, but can now be found in most areas of the country. It is caused by a spirochete type of bacteria most commonly spread among people and animals by the deer tick, *Ixodes dammini,* although it has been reported in other ticks as well.

In dogs, Lyme disease causes arthritis-type symptoms and lameness, fever, loss of appetite, enlarged lymph nodes and kidney disease. In people, Lyme disease first appears as a rash that looks like a bullseye.

If untreated, the disease progresses to cause heart problems and arthritis-type symptoms, especially in the knees, wrists and ankles. Most cases of Lyme disease respond well to antibiotic treatment, although treatment may take months to complete.

Tick paralysis is more commonly seen in dogs than it is in people, although it can affect humans. Tick paralysis occurs when a female tick attaches to the dog and begins to feed. She injects a neurotoxin that causes paralysis that progresses over time, usually seven to nine days. If the tick is removed, the paralysis fades fairly rapidly. However, if the tick is not found and remains on the dog, death can result from respiratory paralysis.

Although some flea products are advertised as also being able to kill ticks, unfortunately, ticks are more difficult to kill than fleas. The best control is to examine your dog daily, running your hands over her—every square inch of her body—and feeling for any bumps. A tick that is full of blood can be as big as the eraser on a pencil, but most are smaller and will feel like a small, flat bump that will be imbedded in the dog's skin. Smear a thick coating of Vaseline over the tick and grab it with a piece of paper towel or toilet paper as it backs out of the dog's skin. If the tick doesn't back out, use a pair of tweezers to gently pull it out of the skin. Grasp the tick with the tweezers as close to the dog's skin as possible, and pull gently and steadily—it could take a few moments.

When you've removed the tick, look at it to make sure the head is attached. If the head has broken off and is still in the skin, an infection or abscess may result and you will need to talk to your vet. Then kill the tick by burning it or by drowning it in alcohol; don't flush it down the toilet—ticks can live under water for a long time. Never use your fingers to remove a tick; the dangers of being exposed to a disease are too great. For the same reason, never kill a tick by squishing it between your fingers. Kill the tick by dropping it in alcohol for a few minutes and then flushing it down the toilet. Do not flush a live tick—it will survive!

Put some antibiotic ointment on the wound in your dog's skin and wash your hands.

If your dog has a tick or flea infestation, you may wish to spray your house or yard with insecticides. Talk to a veterinarian and a groomer before you do. There are many products on the market that can kill these insect pests, but they can also kill everything else; you, your dog, your other pets and the local wildlife. Find a product that will do what you want but will be safe for you and everyone around you. Then follow the directions for that product very carefully.

Internal Parasites

Roundworms are long, white worms (*Toxocara spp*). They are common internal parasites, especially in puppies, although they are occasionally found in adult dogs and people. The adult female roundworm can lay up to 200,000 eggs a day, which are passed out in the dog's feces. Roundworms can only be transmitted via the feces. Because of this, stools should be picked up daily and your dog should be prevented from investigating other dogs' feces.

If dealt with early, roundworms in adult dogs are not serious. However, a heavy infestation can severely affect a dog's health. Puppies with roundworms will not thrive and will appear thin, with a dull coat and a pot belly. You should be able to see worms in the dog's stool if it is infested.

In people, roundworms can be more serious. Therefore, early treatment, regular fecal checks and good sanitation are important, both for your dog's continued good health and yours.

Hookworms (*Unicinaria* and *Ancylostoma*) live their adult lives in the small intestines of dogs. They attach to the intestinal wall and suck blood. When they detach and move to a new location, the old wound continues to bleed because of the anticoagulant the worm injects when it bites. Because of this, bloody diarrhea is usually the first sign of a problem.

Hookworm eggs are passed through the feces and are either picked up from stools, as with roundworms, or, if conditions are right, hatch in the soil and attach themselves to the feet of their new hosts, where they then burrow into the skin. After burrowing through the skin they migrate to the intestinal tract, where the cycle starts all over again.

People can pick up hookworms, too, often by walking barefoot in infected soil. In the Sunbelt states, children often pick up hookworm eggs when playing outside in the dirt or in a sandbox. Treatment, for both dogs and people, may have to be repeated.

Tapeworms attach to the intestinal wall to absorb nutrients. They grow by creating new segments, and usually the first sign of an infestation is when you see rice-like segments in your dog's stool or on its coat near the rectum. Tapeworms are acquired when the dog eats an intermediate host; the most common host is the flea. Therefore, a good flea control program is the best way to prevent a tapeworm infestation.

Whipworms live in the large intestine, where they feed on blood. The eggs are passed in the stool and can live in the soil for many years. If your dog eats the fresh spring grass or buries his bone in the dirt, he can pick up eggs from infected soil. If you garden, you can pick up eggs under your fingernails, infecting yourself when you touch your face.

Heavy infestations cause diarrhea, often watery or bloody. The dog may appear thin and anemic, with poor coat. Severe bowel problems may result from an infestation. Unfortunately, whipworms can be difficult to detect as the worms do not continually shed eggs. Therefore a stool sample one day may be clear while one the next day may show eggs. A single negative stool sample does not mean that your dog does not have whipworms, it simply means no eggs were present in that sample. If you suspect whipworms, have your dog retested.

Giardiasis is caused by the parasitic protozoa, *Giardia*. It is common in wild animals in many areas, so if you take your dog camping or hiking and she drinks from a stream, she could pick it up, just as you can. Diarrhea is usually one of the first symptoms. If the dog has diarrhea, make sure you tell your veterinarian that you and your dog have been camping so that he can test for giardiasis.

Heartworms live in the upper heart and greater pulmonary arteries, where they damage the vessel walls. Poor circulation results, which in turn damages other bodily functions. Eventually, the heart fails and the dog dies.

The adult worms produce thousands of tiny worms called microfilaria. These circulate throughout the bloodstream until they are sucked up by the intermediary host, a mosquito. The microfilaria go through the larval stages in the mosquito, then are transferred to another dog when the mosquito bites again.

Dogs infected with heartworms can be treated if the problem is caught early. Unfortunately, the treatment itself can be risky and has killed some dogs. However, preventive medications are available that kill the larvae. Heartworm can be diagnosed by a blood test, and a negative result is required before starting the preventive medicine. In many areas of the country heartworm preventives are given year-round throughout a dog's life.

Ask your veterinarian how often your dog should be checked for internal parasites. In some locations, once a year is fine. Other parts of the country, where some parasites are more prevalent, may require more vigilance. In any case, if you see signs of worms, (such as in the dog's stool, vomit, or in the hair around the anus), call your veterinarian right away. Resist the urge to treat worms yourself with over-the-counter preparations.

Emergency First Aid

It is often difficult for many dog owners to decide when they need to call their veterinarian and when they can handle a dog's health problem at home. When you are trying to decide what is wrong with your dog, you will need to play detective. Your dog cannot tell you, "There is a pain right here and I feel like I'm going to throw up." You need to put the puzzle pieces together. If you need to call your veterinarian, you will also have to answer some of his or her questions. First of all, what does your dog look like? What was your first clue something was wrong? Is the dog eating normally? What do his stools look like? Is the dog limping? Where? Is any part of his body swollen or red? Is anything painful? Does the dog have a temperature? (Use a rectal thermometer. Normal is 101 to 102 degrees.) Write down all of these clues and be prepared to tell your vet.

Listed below are some commonly seen problems and some basic advice on how handle them. However, the price of a telephone call to your vet is small compared to the value of your dog's life. When in doubt, call!

Vomiting

Did your dog vomit anything? Was there a foreign body? Pieces of sticks, or garbage? If there are no other symptoms, withhold food for 12 hours and water for several hours. When the vomiting has stopped, offer water in ice cube form or in small quantities. If the vomiting continues for more than 12 hours, call your vet.

Diarrhea

What did the stools look like? Was there mucus? Blood? Was there a foreign body, such as garbage? Have you changed your dog's food? That can cause diarrhea.

Withhold food for 12 hours but do not withhold water, as diarrhea can cause dehydration. Many veterinarians advise owners to give Kaopectate or Pepto-Bismol for diarrhea. Call your vet and ask her opinion, asking also what dosage you should give. If the diarrhea lasts for more than 12 hours, call your vet and save a stool sample for her to examine.

Overheating or Heatstroke

Characterized by rapid or difficult breathing, vomiting, even collapse, you need to act at once if you suspect heatstroke. Immediately place your dog in a tub of cold water, or if a tub is not available, run water from a hose over your dog. Use a rectal thermometer to take his temperature and call your vet immediately. If ice is available, place an ice pack on your dog's head. Encourage your dog to drink some of the cool water. Transport the dog to your vet as soon as you can, or as soon as your vet recommends it.

Fractures

Because your dog will be in great pain, you should muzzle him using a soft cloth or a pair of pantyhose. (Wrap the pantyhose around his muzzle and then tie it behind his head.) Do not attempt to set the fracture, but try to immobilize it, if possible, by splinting it with a piece of wood and then wrapping it with gauze or another pair of pantyhose. If there is a board or a door you can use as a backboard or a stretcher so the injured limb is stable, do it. Transport your dog to your veterinarian as soon as you can, moving the dog as little as possible.

Snakebite

Without getting bitten yourself, try to look at the snake, making note of colors, markings and patterns so you or your vet can identify the snake. Keep your dog as quiet as possible to restrict the flow of venom. If the bite is on a leg, apply a soft tourniquet above the would, but make sure it is loosened every three to five minutes. If your dog is in pain or is frantic, muzzle her. Call your vet immediately.

Poisoning

Symptoms of poisoning include retching and vomiting, diarrhea, salivation, labored breathing, dilated pupils, weakness, collapse or convulsions. Sometimes one or more symptoms will appear, depending upon what was ingested or inhaled. If you suspect your dog has been in contact with something poisonous, time is critical. Call your veterinarian right away. If your vet is not immediately available, call the Animal Poison Hotline at (800) 548-2423. The hotline and your vet will need to know what your dog ingested and how much. Do not make your dog vomit unless instructed to do so.

Animal Bites

Muzzle your dog if she is in pain. Trim the hair from around the wound and then liberally pour hydrogen peroxide over it. A hand-held pressure bandage can help stop the bleeding. Call your vet as soon as possible, as he may want to see the dog.

Stitches may be necessary if the bite is a rip or gash, and the vet may recommend putting your dog on antibiotics.

Bleeding

If your dog is in pain, muzzle him. Place a gauze pad, or if that is not available, a clean terrycloth towel, over the wound and apply pressure. If the wound will require stitches or if bleeding does not stop, call your vet right away. If the wound is on a leg and continues to bleed, a soft tourniquet can be applied but make sure it is loosened every three to five minutes.

Choking

If your dog is pawing at his mouth, gagging, coughing, drooling or has collapsed, immediately open his mouth and look down his throat. If an object is visible, pull it out using your fingers, tweezers or a pair of pliers. If you cannot see the object or cannot pull it out, hit your dog behind the neck or between the shoulders to try and dislodge it. If this fails, try a Heimlich maneuver, adapted for dogs. Grasp either side of your dog's ribcage and apply quick, firm pressure. Repeat.

If your dog can get some air around the obstruction, get him to your vet as soon as possible. If your dog cannot get air around the obstruction, you don't have time to move the dog. Work on getting the object out of his throat.

Drowning

Pull your dog out of the water and hold her up by the back legs (if you are strong enough), allowing any inhaled water to drain from her lungs. Remove any foreign matter from her throat. If your dog isn't breathing, pull her tongue to the side of her mouth, close her muzzle and breathe into her nose. Watch her chest for breaths. Repeat until your dog will breathe on her own or until you can get her to the vet.

Other Health Problems

Hip Dysplasia is a disease of the coxofemoral joint; to put it simply, it is a failure of the head of the femur (thigh bone) to fit into the acetabulum (hip socket). Hip dysplasia is not simply caused by poorly formed or positioned bones; many researchers believe it is linked somehow to the formation of hip joint osteoarthritis, also known as degenerative joint disease. Hip dysplasia primary affects certain larger breeds, and research is continuing.

Hip dysplasia is considered to be a polygenic inherited disorder, which means many different genes may lead to the disease, not just one. Also, environmental factors may lead to hip dysplasia, including nutrition and exercise, although the role environmental factors play in the disease is hotly debated among experts.

Hip dysplasia can cause a wide range of problems, from mild lameness to movement irregularities to crippling pain. Dogs with hip dysplasia must often limit their activities, may need corrective surgery or may even need to be euthanized because of the pain.

Contrary to popular belief, hip dysplasia cannot be diagnosed by watching a dog run or by the way it lies down; hip dysplasia can only be accurately diagnosed with an X-ray. Once the X-ray is taken, it can be sent to the Orthopedic Foundation of America (OFA), which grades and certifies the X-rays of dogs over the age of two years (OFA, University of Missouri, Columbia, MO 65211). Sound hips are rated excellent, good or fair, and the dog's owner will receive a certificate with the rating. A dysplastic dog will be rated as mild, moderate or severe. Since the problem is genetic, a dog that has been found to be dysplastic should be spayed or neutered.

Bloat is the acute dilation of the stomach, caused when the stomach fills with gas and air and swells. This swelling of the stomach puts pressure on all the organs in the dog's abdomen, including the diaphragm, which can make it difficult for the animal to breathe. Pressure on the veins returning blood to the heart traps blood in the dog's back end and keeps blood from returning to the heart to be repumped. This causes shock or heart failure, both of which can cause death. Bloat can also cause torsion, where the stomach turns or twists on its long axis, again causing shock and death.

The first symptoms of bloat are obvious. The dog will be pacing and panting, showing signs of distress. The dog's sides will begin to distend. To be successful, treatment should begin at once—there is no time for any delay. If the pressure is not immediately relieved, death can follow within an hour.

Bloat is seen most often in large, deep-chested breeds. To prevent bloat, do not allow your dog to drink large quantities of water after exercising or after eating and limit exercise for a couple of hours after eating.

• •

CHAPTER 14

As Your Dog Grows Older

Most breeds live, on the average, 14 years, although a dog's life span depends on many factors, including its breed, size and general health. However, to live that long, remaining healthy and happy, your dog will need your help. Aging in dogs, as in people, brings some problems. You will probably see your dog's vision dim, her hearing fade and her joints stiffen. Heart and kidney disease are common in old dogs. Reflexes will not be as sharp as they were and your dog may be more sensitive to heat and cold. Your dog may also get grouchy, showing less tolerance for younger dogs, children and other things that are not part of her normal routine.

An old dog that has lived with you most of his adult life is a special gift. Your old dog knows your ways, your likes and dislikes and your habits. He seems almost able to read your mind and his greatest joy is to be close to you. Your old dog will, however, need your care to help him through his old age comfortably.

The Veterinarian, Again

Now, more than ever, you will need to forge a strong relationship with a veterinarian you trust. Your dog's veterinarian will need to get to know your dog, know what is normal and what isn't so that as your dog ages, the vet will see the changes in your dog.

At some point during your dog's middle to late adult years, your vet will want to run some tests, probably including a blood work up, so that he or she can establish a baseline of what is going on in your dog's body. Then, as your dog ages, more recent tests can be compared to the early tests, giving your vet a better idea of what is happening. Obviously, these tests cost money, but they are a good investment for your dog's health.

Although no one has discovered a cure for old age, many of the problems of old age can be helped, either by changing your routine, by assisting your dog in some way or by working with your veterinarian.

Arthritis is common in old dogs. The joints get stiff, especially when it's chilly. Your dog may have trouble jumping or getting up in the morning. Warmth can help arthritis. A warm, comfortable bed might help your dog wake up a little more limber and a little less sore. Talk to your veterinarian about treatment; there are pain relievers that can help.

As your dog's activity level slows down he will need to consume fewer calories, and as his body ages, your dog will need less protein. However, your dog's body may be less able to process and digest the food he eats and this may show up in a poor coat or stools. A heaping tablespoon of yogurt containing live, active cultures can help his digestion, and several of the premium grade dog food manufacturers produce foods specially formulated for old dogs.

Your dog may need to have her teeth cleaned professionally and this is something that cannot be put off. Bacteria that harden and build up on the teeth, called plaque, can infect the gums, get into the bloodstream and cause infections in other parts of the body, including the heart and kidneys. Talk to your veterinarian about a dental cleaning. For dogs this is done under anesthesia, so he or she may recommend a blood workup first to see how your dog's kidneys, liver and other organs are functioning before putting your dog under.

Exercise is still important to your old dog. He needs the stimulation of moving around and of seeing and smelling the world. However, the exercise must be tailored to your dog's needs and abilities. If your dog can still chase the Frisbee, let him. But if you know that jumping causes pain, throw the Frisbee low and flat so that your dog can catch it without jumping.

If your dog is capable only of going for a walk, do that. Let your old dog set the pace and protect her from extremes of weather and stray dogs.

If your dog is going deaf, start to use more hand signals. If she looks confused at what you are asking her to do, smile and help her. Many old dogs get confused and afraid and do not need corrections or scoldings; instead, be patient.

If your dog is incontinent, talk to your veterinarian. Sometimes medication can help. Otherwise, have your dog sleep on an absorbent pad or wear diapers. Don't scold him for that puddle or bowel movement; he can't help it.

As your dog progresses into old age, he may get weak and may have trouble getting up. Help him as much as you can without stripping him of his dignity.

If you use herbal or homeopathic remedies yourself, you may be interested in learning that many people use them for their dogs as well. Many people recommend vitamin C for dogs with arthritis. Rose hips, also a good source of vitamin C, aid the digestion, as does yogurt (mentioned in Chapter 12). Chamomile tea is calming and is good for an upset stomach. Yucca is a natural anti-inflammatory and is wonderful for aches and pains, as well as for arthritis.

For more information, check at your library for books on herbal medicine. *The Holistic Guide for a Healthy Dog* by Wendy Volhard and Dr. Kerry Brown (Howell Book House, New York, 1995) and *Natural Health for Dogs* by Richard and Susan Pitcairn (Rodale Press, Emmaus, PA, 1982) are two, and there are many others available.

Sylvia Wins With a Kiss

When Dave and Christy Waehner lost their 13-and-a-half-year-old Doberman Pinscher and 11-year-old Greyhound, they were devastated. Christy said, "The house had never seemed so empty. I felt the only way to help ourselves was to find another dog who needed lots of love. Naturally, a rescue came to mind."

The Waehners visited Judith Fellton of North Metro Doberman Rescue in Marietta, Georgia, and met Sylvia when she bounded into the room, showering them with, as Christy calls it, "Doberkisses." Sylvia, a 14-month-old spayed, gorgeous Doberman Pinscher, went home with the Waehners the following day and settled in wonderfully.

Sylvia has since attended a Canine Good Citizen class and passed the graduation test. She is now attending a Novice Obedience class and her new owners say she is a willing and eager worker and feel that her future is unlimited.

Christy said, "Would we do this again? You bet! I think rescue dogs develop a special bond with those who give them a second

When It's Time to Say Good-Bye

We have the option not to let our dogs suffer when they are old, ill and infirm. There will come a time when you will need to decide how you are going to handle making this most difficult decision. Some people feel that the time has come when the dog is no longer enjoying life, when he is incontinent and despondent because he has broken house-training, when he's too weak to stand or when the bad days outnumber the good days. Only you can make the decision, but spare your dog the humiliation of incontinence, convulsions, or the inability to stand up or move.

If your old dog must be helped to her death, your veterinarian can give an injection that is an overdose of anesthetic. Your dog will go to sleep and quietly stop breathing. Be there with your dog. Let your arms hold your old friend and let your dog hear your

chance. There seems to be a sense of gratitude for the new oppor-
tunity to shine. It's great to see them blossom."

To rescue a Doberman in your area, call the Doberman
Pinscher Club of America's rescue coordinator at (404) 971-1533.

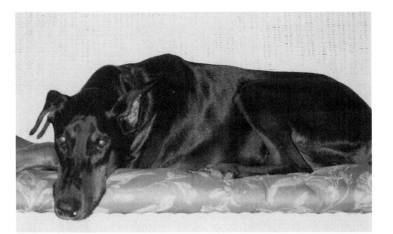

Sylvia is the second rescue dog for David and Christy Waehner.
(Courtesy of Christy Waehner)

voice saying how much you love her as she goes to sleep. There will
be no fear and the last thing your dog will remember is your love.

A well-loved dog is an emotional investment with unparalleled
returns. Unfortunately, our dogs' lives are much too short and we
must learn to cope with inevitable loss. Grief is a natural reaction
to the loss of a loved one, whether it is a pet, a spouse, a friend
or a family member. Grief has no set pattern; its intensity and
duration are different for each person and can be different for
each loss.

Sometimes the best outlet for grief is a good, hard cry. For
other people, talking about the pet or your loss is good therapy.
However, don't allow people who say, "But it was only a dog,"
to put you off. Talk to people who own dogs, preferably other
people who have lost an old dog. They understand your grief and
your need to talk.

Ceremonies can be helpful, too, allowing you to say good-bye to your dog and to release some of your grief. Sprinkling your dog's ashes under a fragrant rose bush or burying him under a favorite apple tree will give you a living monument, a place where you can enjoy nature, where you can recall the wonderful times you shared.

PART IV

The Next Step

CHAPTER 15

• •

Getting Involved With Rescue Work

People begin working with rescue programs for many reasons. Some like the fact that they are saving dogs' lives. Others care about the pet overpopulation problem and want to work towards ending that. Many people are born teachers and like to teach people about dogs. Some like the challenge of fund-raising and have combined a love of their own dog with the needs of breed rescue. The purebred dog rescue movement needs people from all walks of life with many different talents and skills.

If you are already familiar with a local purebred dog rescue group (perhaps the one where you adopted your dog) you may want to give them a call. If you don't know of a rescue group for your breed in your area, check the local humane society or shelter; they may have a listing of the local groups. There is also a discussion of how to find rescue groups in Chapter 4 of this book.

When you have found a local group, ask them what they need and tell them what you might be able to do. If you aren't in a position to foster dogs, you might be able to do some fund-raising, work on the newsletter, make telephone calls, retype care sheets, address envelopes or do one of a thousand other important jobs.

Jobs That Always Need Doing

Most rescue groups maintain a network of foster homes where dogs awaiting adoption can be cared for until a new home is found. In a foster home the dog can be evaluated over a period of time. How is he with other dogs? Does she chase cats? Is he good with other people? Is she house-trained? Is he afraid of brooms, hoses, the vacuum cleaner, men or anything else? Does he accept grooming? Has she had any training? The answers to these and other questions will allow the rescue group to better evaluate the individual dog and to then place him in the appropriate home. The adoptive owner, too, will benefit because she will know more about her new dog.

To foster a dog, you will need to have a secure, fenced-in yard or dog run—both is even better. You will probably want to have an extra kennel crate or two in case you need to confine either your dog, the foster dog, or both. Extra dog equipment is necessary, too, such as food bowls, water bowls, leashes, collars and so on.

Some rescue groups have other requirements. Some prefer homes where at least one person is home all day; others want to know how long the dog will be left alone each day. The Aussie Rescue & Placement Helpline requires that foster home volunteers keep the rescue representatives informed of the progress of each fostered dog. Health problems, behavior issues and training setbacks are all important.

Some rescue groups ask their volunteers to start teaching the dog basic obedience commands. Others require only that the dog walk on a leash, have some house manners and be house-trained. The Border Collie Rescue of Ohio has an active network of foster families who make sure the fostered dog is house-trained and learns basic manners. Because Border Collies are such intense dogs and like to work, the foster families also make sure the dogs have one particular skill that they really enjoy—herding, Agility, Frisbee

Fostering Homeless Dogs

Over the last year Kathy Sullivan has had 17 different dogs living in her home, not all at the same time, and only one has stayed longer than four weeks. Kathy is a dedicated volunteer who takes in homeless dogs selected for potential placement by the German Shepherd rescue group she works with.

Kathy said, "I bring the dog into my home after it has been checked by the veterinarian for good health and has been vaccinated, spayed or neutered. While the dog stays with me, I can watch it and see what it's personality is like, whether it gets along with my resident dog, Jake, and where potential temperament problems might surface. I can also start some obedience training so that the dog can go to a new home with some manners. And if it's not house-trained, of course, I take care of that, too."

"By fostering these dogs, I feel I serve as a bridge for the dog between its old situation and its new family. I can tell the family that their dog is good with my dog, great with the cat but seems to be afraid of cars, or brooms or hoses. That way they have fewer surprises to deal with along the way. By staring training before the dog goes to its new home, I can make sure the dog is better prepared for its future life."

Kathy is one of thousands of people who open their homes to homeless dogs for a brief time. Joan Hamilton took in a 10-year-old Newfoundland, Sunny, who had terrible skin problems, had never been spayed, had a tumor on her back leg and had been over-medicated. Working with her veterinarian, Joan had the dog spayed, removed the tumor, cleared up the skin condition and nursed the dog back to health. When Sunny joined the Hamilton's household, she looked every day of her 10 years, if not older. When she left six months later to go to her new home she looked, and acted, at least five years younger.

or flyball—and that the skill is passed on to the dog's new owner. The owners are told to treat this activity as the dog's work, and it must be done regularly so that the dog has a chance to use his working instincts.

Most rescue groups reimburse foster home volunteers for the dog's basic expenses, such as food, vaccinations and spaying or neutering. Any other expenses, such as toys and treats, must be paid for by the volunteer.

If fostering seems like too much to do, there's plenty of other work. People are always needed to answer calls, return calls and provide information about a particular breed. People will call who have done some research and are serious about adopting a dog, while others will call who have just started thinking about a new dog and may not be familiar with the breed at all. Telephone volunteers will also need information about the rescue process. Rescue volunteers also make calls to check on the references of potential adopters and calls to check up on the progress of newly adopted dogs.

Every organization has some administrative work and needs someone who is very organized to keep track of everything. Files need to be maintained on each dog that goes through the system, each person giving up a dog and each person adopting a dog. Most groups also maintain a network of professionals willing to work with the group—groomers, veterinarians and trainers. Records must be kept concerning all aspects of the group's existence, including the minutes of meetings, bylaws, rules and regulations and more.

Financial records must also be kept, tracking income (donations, fund-raisers and adoptions) and expenses (veterinary bills, reimbursed expenses and more). Financial reports will need to be prepared and made available to the appropriate people.

Most rescue groups apply for non-profit status as soon as they are organized well enough to do so. Not only will this make it cheaper to do business, but it also makes it easier to do fund-raising. The Internal Revenue Service and state tax boards are very specific as to what records must be kept for this tax status, so the person maintaining these records should be familiar with tax laws and accounting or bookkeeping.

Rescue groups should also be incorporated. Incorporation has many benefits, including protecting members of the group and their assets from exposure to liability in the event of a lawsuit. Corporation law can be very complex, however, and legal counsel might be necessary to guide the group through the process. That's why all rescue groups can benefit from good legal counsel, especially someone versed in dog laws. All groups use some form of contract for the old owner to release a dog to the rescue group and a contract for new owners to adopt a dog. These contracts must obviously be legally correct and enforceable. Other legal issues include the group's liability should a dog injure or bite someone while under the rescue group's supervision, or should the dog cause a problem after adoption.

Legal counsel might also be necessary to protect you (or the group) from negligence. If you, or another member of your group makes a mistake and a dog causes injury to someone else, legal protection might be needed. For example, a newly rescued dog might chase cars; if the dog dashes out into the street and causes an accident, the rescue group can be liable.

As mentioned earlier in this book, another on-going need is money. A successful fund-raiser has a very special talent and every non-profit group needs one of these people. There are always more worthwhile organizations requesting money than people have money to give, and a talented fund-raiser can make or break a group. Some rescue groups make money by holding car washes, garage sales and bake sales, while others sponsor picnics, dog walks and even black tie banquets. Even if you don't feel you can come up with fund-raising ideas, you can still help with the organization and leg-work for these events.

To do their work, rescue groups must also be known in their community. Local pet professionals must know that the rescue group is available and be able to guide a desperate dog owner to the group. The group must be known so that volunteers can recruit new volunteers and professionals willing to work with the group. The person in charge of publicity might submit regular publicity releases to the local newspapers, might send in a particularly heart-warming story or might invite the local media to the next fund-raising event.

Someone needs to find potential new owners, needs to mail them an application, needs to interview these people, check out their house, yard and lifestyle and then make a decision as to whether this person (or family) is a potentially good dog owner. Someone needs to process the adoption and follow up later, making sure this new home is working. Someone needs to be available to answer the new owner's questions, both about dogs in general and about this dog in particular.

Someone with a registered, insured vehicle must be able pick up dogs from shelters or from their former owners. Someone needs to deliver the dogs to foster homes or new homes. Someone

---

Kirby, Franz and One Rescue Volunteer

Kate Payne, a member of the Texas Gulf Coast Vizsla Club, works with the group's rescue program and has adopted both Kirby and Franz. She says most Vizslas come into rescue because their owners were not prepared for the breed's temperament; often they simply cannot handle their dog anymore.

Payne says, "Vizslas are truly wonderful dogs, but they are a handful and have pretty complicated temperaments. Their medium size, short coat and affectionate temperament makes them appear to be the ideal family pet. Unfortunately, when people do not see the down side to this breed the dogs will be the ones to suffer."

Franz was Payne's first Vizsla. He was surrendered because he was a fence jumper. When she brought him home, he was also

is often needed to take dogs to the local veterinarians, to the groomers or to the kennel, when necessary.

Most groups publish a newsletter. Sometimes it's just two or three photocopied pages, and sometimes it's a larger, more elaborate, professional looking newsletter or magazine. Volunteers are always needed to help with the newsletter. If you write, draw, take good photographs, can type or have a computer, you can volunteer to help. Or, if you have time to copy, collate, fold, staple, address and stamp newsletters, volunteer to do that.

Veterinarians who wish to help could provide advice, examinations or discounts on services. Dog trainers or obedience instructors could offer help, advice or discounts, as could groomers.

Many rescue groups have tables at local events or dog shows to help spread the word about their group and volunteers are always needed for these events. New volunteers are always needed, too, for these and other aspects of rescue work. People can't

---

an emotional mess. He was afraid of storms, urinated in the house when afraid and was a fear biter. He went through obedience class shortly after adoption and today, at 15 years young, is still going strong (although storms are still worrisome for him).

Kirby was considered unadoptable because of his emotional problems, so Payne kept him herself. She describes his problems as post-traumatic stress disorder and says he is so stressed by crowds of people that he cannot attend obedience classes.

Payne recommends that people thinking about buying or adopting a Vizsla spend some time with a Vizsla in its "native habitat": running through the house, dashing around the yard, climbing trees after birds, shouting, yelling, tumbling and then, only then, lying still for petting.

To find a Vizsla rescue group in your area, call the Vizsla Club of America rescue coordinator at (501) 888-7333.

volunteer until they know about the organization, so people are always needed to spread the word.

What are your talents? What do you like to do? Chances are, you have something valuable to offer a rescue group.

It's Tough to Do It Alone

Do you want to start your own rescue group? Experienced rescue volunteers suggest you really think it through before you try to do this on your own. Katherine Jacobson used to do rescue work by herself and now works with a larger group sponsored by a breed club. She said, "I have seen both sides of the issue and there are good and bad to both. Obviously, if you are doing rescue work by yourself, you are your own boss and many people like that. I sure did. When you work with a larger group, you have to follow someone else's rules and many times that's hard.

"However, when you are working by yourself you have no help. I answered telephone calls at all hours of the night. I drove to pick up dogs, took them to the vet, paid the vet bills myself and then tried to find new homes for all the dogs. I worried about losing my house when a dog bit its new owner and the owner threatened to sue me. I was neglecting my family, myself and my own dogs. When you are working with a larger group, there is always help just a phone call away."

Suzanne Kane, editor of the *Muttmatchers Messenger* newsletter, agrees that rescuing dogs is hard work. In an interview in *Dog Fancy* magazine, Kane said, "Breed rescue requires lots of hard work and a tough skin. It's stressful, demanding, expensive and time-consuming, particularly if the breed you are rescuing is a popular one." Kane suggests working with a rescue group in your area. "Don't try to reinvent the wheel if you don't have to. Don't try to do it all by yourself. An existing club will probably have non-profit status, which will save you money." It will also have an existing network of information and volunteers.

It's also important to remember that rescue work can be very, very difficult. Anyone who has been involved in it will tell you so. Rescue work requires your time and efforts. It is emotionally, physically and financially demanding.

Many people who work in rescue, especially those who rescue some of the more popular breeds like German Shepherds and Rottweilers, can easily become overwhelmed. Maureen Greathouse rescues German Shepherds through the Seattle Purebred Dog Rescue program. In 1989, she processed 18 German Shepherds; in 1995, 371. Not only is this traumatic for the rescuers, but it is awful for the dogs themselves and for the breed. All of the popular breeds face the same problem.

Rescue volunteers also get extremely tired of hearing poor excuses. Margaret Schaeffer also rescues German Shepherds, and asks, "How can someone give up a three-month-old puppy because it isn't house-trained? They haven't even given the poor baby a chance." Gretchen Poorman rescues Doberman Pinschers, "A local family turned in an eight-year-old dog because they are moving." she said. "Why they couldn't they take their dog with them? Don't they realize how much their dog is grieving?" Sara Tennison rescues Cocker Spaniels, and said, "Last week I took in an eight-month-old dog who was given up because she is too rowdy. They were willing to get rid of her but were not willing to exercise her or train her."

Rescuers who have dealt with injured, abused, neglected and sick dogs can easily become overwhelmed with anger. Jennifer Haven rescues Shar-Peis and recently took in a four-month-old cream colored Shar-Pei who had been taken from its owner by a local police officer. "The dog's owner had been kicking her down the street because she had a house-training accident. When I stopped him, the young man said that this was his dog and he could do anything he wanted to her, so I took the dog and arrested him for cruelty to animals," said the police officer.

It is also impossible for any one person, or any one rescue group, to save every dog. And it is always difficult to make that decision to not save a dog; especially when you know that your decision will probably result in that dog's death.

However, when you can save a dog's life all of your work, time and efforts are rewarded. When that dog is placed into a new, responsible, suitable home, you will feel such a sense of satisfaction and relief. Later, when you check up on the dog and you find that the dog is now a well-behaved, well-loved member of the family, don't be surprised if you cry with happiness.

• •

Further Reading

On Health

The Complete Book of Dog Health by William J. Kay,
DVM, Chief of Staff at the Animal Medical Center,
with Elizabeth Randolph (Howell Book House,
New York, 1985)

The Consumer's Guide to Dog Food by Liz Palika
(Howell Book House, New York, 1996)

The Dog Owner's Home Veterinary Handbook by Delbert
Carlson, DVM, and James Giffin, MD (Howell
Book House, New York, 1992)

Guide to Skin and Haircoat Problems in Dogs by Lowell
Ackerman (Alpine Publications, Loveland, CO,
1994)

Help! The Quick Guide to First Aid for Your Dog by
Michelle Bamberger, DVM (Howell Book House,
New York, 1995)

Old Dogs, Old Friends by Bonnie Wilcox, DVM,
and Chris Walkowicz (Howell Book House,
New York, 1991)

The Well Dog Book by Terri McGinnis (Random
House, New York, 1991)

On Training

DogPerfect by Sarah Hodgson (Howell Book House, New York, 1996)

Dog Problems by Carol Lea Benjamin (Howell Book House, New York, 1989)

Dog Training in 10 Minutes by Carol Lea Benjamin (Howell Book House, 1996)

Good Owners, Great Dogs by Brian Kilcommons and Sarah Wilson (Warner Books, New York, 1992)

Kids + Dogs = Fun by Jacqueline O'Neil (Howell Book House, New York, 1996)

Making Friends: Training Your Dog Positively by Linda Colflesh (Howell Book House, New York, 1990)

Second Hand Dog by Carol Lea Benjamin (Howell Book House, New York, 1988)

What All Good Dogs Should Know by Jack Volhard and Melissa Bartlett (Howell Book House, New York, 1991)